MORE ADVANCE PRAISE FOR
WHAT DO I DO NOW?

• • •

"Shena Crane has clearly and succinctly identified the fundamental challenges for all segments of today's workforce. The world of work as we have known it in the past is, indeed, rapidly changing. Sadly, neither business nor education has successfully interpreted what these changes mean to the individual worker. This handbook will be invaluable to everyone faced with seeking first-time employment or added career options."

— Evelyn Brown Lee, Member, Board of Regents; State of Utah; Former Director of Economic Development Division, State of Utah

• • •

"Shena Crane offers us up-to-the-minute information about careers, work and jobs—and outlines exciting strategies for career and job changers as they meet the challenges of the new workplace. Motivating—and very readable!"

— Pat Nellor Wickwire, Ph.D., President; American Assn. for Career Education

• • •

"I found the book informative, and containing the basic tools necessary for making a plan of attack for career changes and understanding the important elements of the workplace."

— Jane Rogers, International Military Community Executives Association

• • •

"*What Do I Do Now?* is a timely book offering a fresh, easy-to-use approach to career planning. Crane's understanding of current workplace trends, along with examples and practical information makes this book a must for anyone in the throes of or anticipating a career change."

— Maria Laqueur, Executive Director; Assn. of Part-Time Professionals

• • •

"As a wheelchair mobile executive of an employment agency for people with disabilities, I am encouraged by Ms. Crane's book. I strongly urge human resources professionals and hiring managers to read it and pass it on! *What Do I Do Now?* conveys a clear and positive message to employers that ability is all it takes."

— *Mikki Lam, Executive Director; Just One Break, Inc.*

• • •

"It presents a realistic view of today's marketplace and . . . is reader friendly. . . . There are plenty of good ideas for those seeking to move up in their present organization or make a change. The entire book is pertinent."

— *Doyle Manning, Former Baxter Healthcare Human Relations Executive*

• • •

"Everyone's ego is put through the wringer as you try to convince an employer that you'll earn your pay for the job that's offered. The special challenges of applicants with a disability compound the anxiety of the job search. I'm very grateful to Ms. Crane for addressing these challenges in this book."

— *Miriam Whitfield, Employment Specialist; Social Vocational Services (Los Angeles)*

WHAT DO I DO NOW?

Making Sense
of Today's
Changing Workplace

SHENA CRANE

VISTA PRESS
Irvine, California

Cover and text design by Eula Palmer

Printed in the United States of America

10 9 8 7 6 5 4 3

Publisher's Cataloging in Publication
(Prepared by Quality Books Inc.)

Crane, Shena R.
    What do I do now? : making sense of today's changing workplace / Shena Crane.
    p. cm.
    Includes bibliographical references and index.
    Preassigned LCCN: 93-94164
    ISBN 0-9638247-0-8

    1. Vocational guidance--United States. 2. Success in business.
I. Title.

HF5381.C73 1993   650.1
                                    QBI93-1276

DEDICATED TO MOLLY SINGER

Acknowledgments

Acknowledgments and thanks usually start with professional relationships and end with family and friends. But in my case, these distinctions blur. The effort to conceive and write this book could not have begun without the foundation and wholeness created by some very special people in my life to whom I give my thanks and love . . .

To my husband Barry Bauling, the best a person can be in this world, whose ideas, thoughts and comments sparked the creation of this book and whose patience and humor helped bring it to fruition.

To my stepdaughters Tami Bauling and Erin Bauling, whose love and friendship have expanded my life to new dimensions of happiness, experience and emotion.

To Judy Cooper, my editor, who became and remained my friend despite the rigors of the process, who coped with my raw thoughts, helped transform them into coherent entities and knew what I wanted to say when I couldn't say it.

To Eula Palmer, my friend and designer, for working with me through the way-back-when original and the swerving, meandering starts of this book and for being an ever-willing interpreter of my less-than-straightforward thought processes.

To my long-time friends, Cathy Thompson, Carol Havens and Kim O'Hair, thanks for providing love and support.

And special thanks and appreciation to Peter Sukin and Peggy Bolks for helping me keep mind and body together during the process.

And finally, to my mom Molly Singer, the first to believe in me and who would tell me of her pride in me if she were alive; sometimes I think I hear her say it anyway.

CONTENTS

PART THREE: PAVING NEW GROUND

PART FOUR: SPECIAL ADVICE FOR SPECIAL GROUPS

PART ONE:
A VIEW FROM ABOVE

1. EVERYTHING IS DIFFERENT

What Planet *Is* This?

You hear it everywhere: "What do I do now?" It is the cry of millions of confused Americans trying to figure out what's going on in today's unrecognizable workplace. What happened to the jobs, the companies, the careers they were supposed to have? Many feel as if they have landed on a new planet and are stumbling over unfamiliar terrain.

Actually, thinking of today's workplace as "unfamiliar terrain" is pretty accurate. White-collar workers have been hard hit by recessionary times, with 3.1 million unemployed as of June 1993. The 1990-1991 recession was the first in which white-collar job growth declined, with new positions being created at half the rate of those of previous recessions. In the past, many laid-off white-collar workers could count on new job growth to rescue them from unemployment—now their plight is often extended or even permanent.

Blue-collar workers, who always suffer during hard times, are also being affected with permanent layoffs. When white- and blue-collar positions are combined, 85 percent of the total layoffs from the 1990-1991 recession are estimated to be permanent, as opposed to 56 percent in the prior four recessions, leaving much of the workforce out in the cold.[1]

And more layoffs are on the horizon: In 1993, over one-third of the corporations that had downsized in the last five years were expected to do so again within the year.[2]

Attitude Adjustment Required

Even when faced with facts like these, most people prefer to think of today's job climate as *a time to be gotten through* until things *return to normal*, businesses *go back to the way they were* and career paths *advance the way they are supposed to*. It isn't going to happen.

Buying into these myths is neither realistic nor helpful. Today, in order to do well, or just survive, people must revise their ideas about careers, and jobs. Those who continue to plan careers and pursue jobs based on yesterday's realities will have a tough time succeeding.

Adopting the "stranger-in-a-strange-land" perspective helps in coping with the radical changes that have occurred. Since you don't know the terrain, it's best to look it over with an open mind before charting your course of action. Managing your career in the 1990s means:

- **Accepting and positively dealing with change.**
- **Being receptive to previously nonexistent or unconsidered options.**
- **Thinking of your career as a process that reveals itself as it happens.**

To do this, you need to "rethink" the way you view your career, recognize when old premises are no longer appropriate and replace them with new assumptions that reflect today's workplace.

This may not be a comfortable process. Any type of change can be painful, and career change is no exception. But in the long run you will be doing yourself a favor by changing your mind-set—you will make better decisions because they will be based on what is really happening. Not changing your thinking is like keeping an old rotary-dial phone, rather than replacing it with a touch-tone. The rotary phone makes it a lot harder to communicate because it is out of sync with everyone else's systems.

Getting and staying in sync with what is going on will allow you to be successful in today's new workplace. And the first step to getting in sync is to understand how career paths have changed.

A Brief History of Careers

In the past, people who moved from one career to another were regarded as unstable, indecisive, even flaky. Raised by parents influenced by the Great Depression, most were brought up believing that you picked a career, trained for it (or were trained on the job) and found a position in your chosen field. Then, for the rest of your life, you stayed in the same career. If you were lucky, you even remained with the same company, advancing up its corporate ladder.

By the 1970s, the concept of what constituted an ideal career path began to change. Despite periodic recessions, overall strong economic growth had resulted in an abundance of jobs, especially in new fields and technologies. At the same time, career attitudes were affected by the "hippie" movement of the late 1960s and early 1970s. While proportionately few people in the country actually dropped out and wore flowers in their hair, many did begin to ask themselves if they liked their work, if they felt fulfilled, if it was worthwhile. These questions gave birth to an attitude of entitlement, a belief that *people should be able to have jobs they like and not be stuck in jobs they don't like.* While the predominance of this belief varied, overall, a sense of "entitlement" prevailed.

Throughout the prosperity of the middle and late 1980s, the entitlement attitude persisted and sprouted another new concept about work: *People should have the freedom to change careers if they want to.* If you didn't like what you did, or had grown tired of it, or had identified something new you wanted to do, you should be able to make a switch. Dramatic changes began to occur as many abandoned careers like pharmacy, teaching or corporate management to become sales representatives, travel agents or fitness instructors.

Next, both the ideas of liking what you do for a living and having the choice to change what you do became supported by another belief—*that different people like to do different things and that this is okay.*

I recall chatting with a client who had become a good friend. She asked, "If you could just do anything you wanted, what would you do?" "I'd sing," I confided, "I'd be a rock star." She raised her brows in surprise and said "Oh." I returned the question, "Well, what would you do?" She got a faraway look and mused, "I'd go into solid waste management." Equally mystified, I remarked, "Really?" While we laughed at each other's choices, we agreed that people had the right to make different choices without any value judgments being made.

As the 1980s progressed, American workers continued to strive for the "good life." *Ambition is good and more ambition is even better* became another tenet in the work world. Armed with higher education, presented with enormous career opportunities and outfitted with credit cards, the baby boomers became the generation that wanted it all and believed they would get it. Both women and men shifted their careers into hypergear, working like crazy to climb the corporate ladder, make their mark and fulfill the American Dream. This attitude was only somewhat, if at all, exaggerated by actor Michael Douglas, who, in the role of business tycoon Gordon Gekko in the movie *Wall Street*, proclaimed "Greed is good."[3] People became comfortable with the notion that you could fulfill your spiritual values, have power and make money at the same time, and still be a good person.

The Art of Rethinking

Most people have spent a great part of their careers maneuvering in this relatively "easy" world defined by entitlement, choice, abundance and ambition. So for most, suddenly hitting the reefs along the rocky career beaches of the 1990s has been a terrible jolt. No one is prepared, no one has a life jacket. No one even imagined a life jacket would be needed.

Nearly everyone is astonished by the changes that have happened in the workplace. Employers are laying off employees before they even have the chance to tire of their jobs and proactively search for greener pastures. Corporate fast-trackers are finding the rungs of the corporate ladder collapsing beneath the Nikes they wore while cramming in a workout during their lunch hour. Bewildered lifetime careerists at large organizations such as IBM and Eastman Kodak are out the door before a gold watch and pension were ever in sight.

The effect on individual career paths is dramatic as the American workplace continues to change, causing the womb-to-tomb concept of careers to disappear. Virtually everyone will be making career changes. College graduates are predicted to have at least a dozen jobs and change fields three or four times during their work lives.[4] And such switches are not limited to the newly educated. Career and job changers range from recent entrants into the workforce, whose companies restructured during their second year of employment, to workers in their thirties, watching corporate opportunity vanish, to older employees, forced to take early retirement while still needing or wanting to maintain their salary level or simply remain active in the workforce. Age, position or salary offer no protection from having to make a change.

Some career changes will be made by choice. You will decide that you have gone as far as you can with your current employer or you are interested in working with a new technology that has hit the market. Other changes will be involuntary, especially as you work longer and are affected by ongoing organizational restructurings, increasing global competition, the obsolescence of current industries and the growth of new ones resulting from emerging technologies.

Either way, you will find that the choice to remain with a single company, industry or even career is a rare luxury. Today, the real choice isn't whether or not to make changes.

Rather, the only choice is to assume responsibility for change, for managing your own career and ensuring, to the best of your ability, that the steps you take create a sensible career path that allows you to adapt and progress. "If things are changing, you can stay stuck and be changed on top of. Or you can change with things and try to come out on top," says attorney Deborah Arron, author of *Running From the Law*.[5] The latter, assuming control, is obviously the preferable choice.

How you perceive change can determine your success in coping with it. Tough times have transformed many into anxious workers, willing to work for whatever they can get. Overpowered by their fear of change and the loss of a defined career path and worried about everyday realities like money problems, they feel boxed in. They adopt an attitude of simply being grateful if they have or can find a salaried position.

Others, a large group actually, welcome career transformations resulting from the changed workplace. This group, whether unemployed, feeling the threat of unemployment or still working but dissatisfied, see a value in making changes in their lives. Even those who have been asked to leave view it *as a catalyst for new opportunities.*

This kind of can-do attitude is necessary to overcome difficult situations. Many of the unemployed who welcome change are *not* backed with the resources of a large savings account. They usually don't have any more financial security than anyone else. But they face reality and then act upon it. They accept the fact that the only constant may be change itself. These are the people Daniel Valentino, a managing director with Gemini Consulting, is speaking about when he says, "There's an awareness that the reinvention of the corporation is going to go on forever. That's a new feeling. Not long ago, executives thought this thing called change was an event."[6] Change is not an isolated event, it is an ongoing process.

Steering Your Career

It is vital to take responsibility and steer your own career in the changed workplace. Don't relinquish control and just let things happen.

Organizations are making decisions that affect employees, but these decisions are based on what is believed to be *right for the business*, not its individual employees. They are called *business decisions*. Individuals must adopt the same philosophy—**think of your career as a "business" and make business decisions for your career**. This will give you a better perspective.

Suppose your company starts laying off staff, eliminates your job but finds another position for you within the company. A good *business decision* would be to accept the new job but to start looking for employment outside of the company, rather than passively staying in your position out of loyalty or a false sense of security. The company could continue to cut back and you could find yourself laid off three months later. Instead, you could immediately put a contingency plan into action, look into what options exist for your next move and *choose* your next move.

Learn to look at your career as an ongoing, evolving process. Vivian Jennings,* a graphic artist, was hired straight out of college into her first job in a corporate marketing department. After two years, she left for a better opportunity, working for an advertising agency as an art director and then senior art director. After four years, her agency lost the account that she worked on, and her team was laid off. She rejoined the corporate world in a marketing management position with a new company and spent a successful nine years with them. Then, her company sold off one of its major product lines. Vivian realized this sale would ultimately affect her job in terms of responsibilities and opportunities. She left the company, but negotiated to consult to them, added a couple of clients and eventually became a one-person advertising shop.

Vivian navigated some tricky career waters. During this time, she went from a corporate employer to a service provider (the agency), back to the corporate world and then went out on her own. While these maneuvers may appear exhausting, they were necessary. Vivian couldn't have predicted any of the events that caused her to make changes, but *she approached each with flexibility and found a "next step" that would continue her career.* This is essential.

As you go through career changes, remember that everyone does something for the first time. So be fearless, explore far-fetched opportunities. Realize that most people do not have the textbook definition of the appropriate background for their career. Not many people have earned exactly the right degree for the work they do or have a seamless career history of steady promotions. Often, there is no right background. The U.S. Department of Labor claims that 50 percent of the jobs that will exist in the year 2000 haven't been created yet.[7] This means that being selected to take on a new role can be based on demonstrated abilities to adapt quickly and learn new things, rather than on past experience.

Organization theorist Peter Drucker aptly summed up the current workplace when he said, "We're in one of those great historical periods that occur every 200 or 300 years when people don't understand the world anymore, when the past is not sufficient to explain the future."[8] While we may not like this condition, it is where we are.

One of my clients became very successful, making his mark in the marketing of financial services. This should have been impossible because he had no college degree, usually an iron-clad prerequisite for entering this field. But he was bright, extremely personable and very persistent. We worked together off and on for several years, during which time he made two job changes. The last move was to a very substantial marketing position with a prominent brokerage firm. A few months after he started, he brought in his first large investor, and we had lunch to celebrate. When I proposed a toast, he interrupted and blurted out, "You know, sometimes I look at where I am and I think, 'This is amazing. What do I know?' I was in this meeting the other day, the one to close the deal. There was part of me that was standing back and watching me, and I saw that I was smart and knew what I was talking about, and I made it happen. And when I walked out I thought, 'Wow, this must be how it works. *Everyone just makes it up as they go along.*'"

While his statement may seem irreverent, it's really a paraphrase of what Drucker was saying, only brought to a more personal level. Change is occurring, no one knows what will happen, but we have to deal with it and figure it out on the way. "The past is not sufficient to predict the future."[9] Take a proactive approach in directing your career. View your career as a process that requires flexibility, creativity and the determination to start anew. Realize that the first part of the answer to "What do I do now?" is to move forward with courage, optimism and a sense of exploration.

---

* *Name and some details have been changed.*

2.

WHAT'S NEW IN THE NEW WORKPLACE

To successfully operate in today's workplace, you need to understand the factors that have created it.

As everyone knows, companies have downsized. They are operating with dramatically reduced numbers of employees. Downsizing has affected practically all companies. Even IBM, once thought to be indestructible, has suffered substantial losses and reduced its workforce from 406,000 in 1985 to a leaner 302,000 in 1993.[1] While it first hoped to downsize through attrition and voluntary early retirements, some of its reductions ultimately were the result of actual layoffs, a practice all but forbidden in a corporate culture where "full employment"—meaning lifelong employment—was a basic tenet. "It [full employment] was a religion," says a retired IBM manager. "I tell you, this was like virginity."[2]

The downsizing of American companies like IBM is permanent. Lean has become the operating mode of the 1990s as companies learn to run with fewer employees. The main factors at work in allowing this permanent downsizing are: outsourcing, strategic alliances, advances in technology and an emerging global workplace.

Outsourcing Is In

Outsourcing, contracting out to other companies or individuals for goods or services, has become a popular cost-cutting practice in the new workplace. Outsourcing is often the result of a process called "reengineering." **When companies reengineer, they completely re-examine their products and their operations from the ground up and recreate them.** Nothing is sacred, everything can be changed. Reengineering forces companies to focus on their "core competencies," i.e., what they are really good at doing. The products or services that it then offers are based on this core.[3] "Products are a happy way of capturing [a company's] services," says professor Brian Quinn from Dartmouth's Tuck School of Business.[4] Another result of reengineering is that all functions not directly related to core competencies and product or service offerings are closely examined to see if they need to be performed from inside the company, or if they can be "outsourced"—contracted out to other companies who make this function *their* product or core competency. Outsourcing saves a company money by allowing it to have fewer employees and less investment in equipment and facilities, while putting its capital in critical growth areas like research and development or sales.

Traditionally, functions like data processing, accounting, transportation and advertising have been areas that are commonly contracted out to other companies. But almost any function can be outsourced if it is not part of a company's core competencies. Nike and Reebok have defined their core competencies as designing high-tech, fashionable footwear for sports and fitness and marketing them. Neither regards the actual manufacturing of its products as a core competency and both outsource all production to suppliers in Taiwan, South Korea and other Asian countries. (Nike has one small plant that makes shoe parts; Reebok owns no plants.)[5]

Outsourcing has even led to previously unimagined relationships, with small companies outsourcing to large companies or, even more surprisingly, competitive companies outsourcing to one another. Texas Instruments, for example, is manufacturing computers for small companies like Sun Microsystems and Gateway 2000. IBM's outsourcing includes

computers for Hitachi, PC boards for clone makers and diagnostic systems for Chrysler. Unusual as it is, this kind of
outsourcing has been a boon to the large companies who
sometimes manage to avoid layoffs and plant closures by ser-
vicing these unexpected but lucrative markets. IBM is predicted to earn $500 million in 1993 revenues from its
outsourcing activities; Texas Instruments' are projected at
$225 million.[6]

More Productivity With Fewer Employees

Outsourcing allows companies to get by with fewer employees. The employees they do have generally fall into two
categories. The first group, the *core*, is made up of essential
managers, professionals and technicians. This group is employed full time and its presence and knowledge of the company are essential to the running of the organization.

The second group, the *ring*, ranges from professionals and
technicians, such as marketing and computer experts, to support personnel such as word processors and custodians. The
difference is that workers in the ring may not be full-time,
salaried employees. Instead, they may be hired on a contract
basis for either a specific project (as in the case of an advertising campaign) or for a specific length of time (as in hiring a
cleaning service on a yearly contract).

This change in the number and makeup of employees has
required major rethinking on the part of organizations. While
companies have been accustomed to the convenience of having *all* their employees around *all* the time, they are realizing
that it is an expensive, if not extravagant way to stay staffed.
Companies don't need to keep staff once a project is finished;
they can save money by not paying year-round top salaries
and benefits packages. It may go against tradition, but it
makes more sense and is cheaper to use workers outside of
the organization who are self-employed or who work for specialist contractors and to buy their services only when they
are needed. Charles Handy, workplace trends analyst and
author of *The Age of Unreason*, estimates that 80 percent of

the value of a company's product or service could be produced by people outside of the company.[7]

Spurred Growth in Strategic Alliances

Strategic alliances are really a fancy way of defining strong,
profitable relationships that often grow between a company
and the organizations it is outsourcing to, or between two or
more companies with symbiotic core competencies which,
when combined, can produce new products, services or technologies. In either form, the relationship is a profitable strategy for all partner companies as they join forces, with each
contributing what it does best. AT&T, for example, used
Japan's Marubeni Trading Co. to link up with Matsushita
Electronic Industrial Co. to jump-start the production of its
Safari notebook computer, which was designed by Henry
Dreyfuss Associates. MCI Communications Corp. has instituted partnerships with as many as 100 companies to help
them win major contracts with large customers.[8] Arch rivals
IBM and Apple Computer have formed Taligent, a joint software venture to develop a new operating system to compete
with Microsoft and Next, the company started by Apple cre-
ator Steve Jobs.[9]

Expanding Demand for Computer Competency

Improved and expanded technology also has allowed companies to run with fewer employees. In the past, the purpose
of many jobs in an organization was to collect, possess and
analyze data and make decisions based on this data. "Data-
involving" jobs can range from decision-making management
positions to data-entry and inventory clerks. But now, key
information is being made available to more employees, decision-making is being pushed down to lower levels in the organization and, as a result, fewer managers and workers are
necessary. Purchasing, for example, has become a simpler
and faster process at many large retailers. Sales and inventory data, instantaneously recorded with bar codes and laser
scanners at sophisticated "cash registers," can be electroni-

cally sent directly to a key decision-maker on a daily or even hourly basis. This eliminates the need for multi-levels of employees performing data entry, inventory management and market analysis as part of the purchasing process.

Technology is also causing some jobs to become either obsolete or unnecessary as companies find they can maintain or even increase productivity while using fewer employees. Nucor, a steel maker, can make a ton of steel using less than one-twelfth of the labor required 10 years ago.[10] John Mazur, a 50-year-old sheet metal worker says, "Now 10 men can produce as much as 60 to 100 men did 30 years ago, when I got into the business."[11] Even new products may not require substantial labor additions. When Chrysler Corp. invested $225 million in a new line of Dodge Trucks, it only needed to add 70 new jobs.[12]

Another effect of new technologies is that often the products they produce are less labor-intensive (and less material-intensive). Compare, for example, the amount of labor required to build an automobile and the relatively smaller amount needed to make a microprocessor chip used to operate many of the automobile's systems.[13]

The Growing Global Workplace

Today many workers in this country are competing for jobs on a global basis, as companies move more and more work out of the United States. Larry Irving, an executive for Daniels Industries who moved from Houston to run a factory his company bought in Germany, says, "The average American doesn't realize that there is a truly competitive workforce out there that is vying for their jobs. The rest of the world is catching up."[14]

Most of us are aware of the movement of manufacturing jobs and facilities out of the U.S. by companies seeking to reduce capital investments and labor costs, but may not know that service jobs are also being moved out of the country. In Jamaica, 3,500 people work at office parks connected to the

U.S. by satellite dishes. They make airline reservations and process tickets, handle calls to toll-free numbers and perform data entry. Quarterdeck Office Systems, a California-based software company, has its daily customer service calls handled by employees in Dublin, Ireland. (Actually, a lot of calls are being handled in Ireland. The Irish government has educated its workers and spent billions of dollars to upgrade the country's phone system so that the island can function as a telecommunications-based service center.) Companies who need data-entry services are using "typing mills" in the Philippines which charge 50 cents for 10,000 characters (the equivalent of five, double-spaced pages) or take advantage of an even better deal in China where the price is 20 cents. The United States is not alone in moving labor outside of its borders. European and Japanese companies are doing the same. British-owned Reebok uses computer programmers in Bangalore; Swissair has English-speaking certified accountants in Bombay.[15]

Many factors have combined to create the new global workplace. Other countries are making successful efforts to improve their educational systems so that their workers can be competitive. Emerging nations in Latin America and Asia are new growth markets that companies want to penetrate. Previously sequestered countries like China are putting themselves into the world marketplace and workplace. All of these factors take on added significance when combined with the fact that modern technology is allowing companies to place work and workers where they want to, freeing their dependence on location for materials or labor. Hoover Institution economist Milton Friedman says that technology, ". . . makes it possible to produce a product anywhere, using resources from anywhere, by a company located anywhere, to be sold anywhere."[16]

The global workplace is not only causing many American workers to literally compete with workforces in other countries for jobs, it is, in some cases, affecting salary levels. "Very dramatically, jobs are being priced to an international standard. In particular, blue-collar jobs are being marked down to a price that's globally competitive," states Edward E. Lawler II, founder of the USC Center for Effective Organizations.[17]

Career Portfolio Packaging

How does the average American deal with global competition, reduced workforces and the other characteristics of the changing workplace? A good first step is to realize that like companies, individuals must learn to repeatedly *reinvent, package and market themselves as products in the changed work world.*

Marilyn Moats Kennedy, career consultant, states, "The only security for today's migrant managers and professionals is in the *portfolio* of skills they can sell."[18] *Portfolio-ing* is an important new concept that helps you define, package and market yourself as a viable product.

Developing a career portfolio means that you take all of the different kinds of work you have done and put them together into groups of skills and experiences that compose your "work portfolio" or "work profile." Your portfolio doesn't just include what is classically thought of as *work* (being an employee), but draws on experiences and skills acquired from all facets of your life.

In *The Age of Unreason*, professor Charles Handy neatly categorizes virtually everything that people do into five different types of "work." The first two types, wage and fee work, are what come to mind when most people think of their work experience. **Wage (or salary) work** means working as an employee in a defined job and being paid for the time that you put in. **Fee work** is work where you are paid a fee for performing a specific project or task for an organization, but are not an employee of the organization, such as the kind of work consultants and freelancers do.

The next three types of work are often not what people think about when they think of work, but they are important in building your work portfolio. There is **volunteer or gift**

work that you do for free, usually for a cause, charity or community. And there is **study work**, which is just that: going to school, to seminars, to employer-provided training and even self-instruction. The fifth and final type of work is **home work**. This encompasses everything people do at home, from cooking to painting the house.[19]

While perhaps different from the kinds of work people might consider putting in their résumé, including these five kinds of work can highlight experiences and skills that expand your portfolio and help you effectively market yourself and steer your career.

Gregory Bates,* 51, was a successful software development engineer. He spent 28 years with his first company and then left for a small company that was developing an innovative, leading-edge product. Ten months into the job, the computer industry began to decline. Gregory's company, stung with sudden cash-flow problems, decided to scrap the new product and focus on its mainstay product lines. Gregory suddenly found himself out in the job market in an industry that was experiencing massive downsizing. He was in a panic. At a loss, he sat down to review his life to see what he had done that could be applied elsewhere. He made some interesting discoveries.

After years of introducing new products and concepts, Gregory had developed strong communication and training skills, and had become expert in introducing change and getting people to understand and accept it. In addition, he had taught three classes at the local community college in the past five years and had been president of his homeowners' association, a role requiring tact, persuasion and patience. When combined, these experiences, which had been acquired through *salary work* (his two company positions), *fee work* (his teaching) and *volunteer work* (his homeowners' association position), enabled him to incorporate *training experience and skills* into his career portfolio. Changing his focus from the computer industry to industries using large data processing systems, he began to remarket himself. Within four months, he had found a job as a regional user systems trainer with a national financial services organization.

Gregory was able to survive a difficult career situation because he realized the predicament he was in and then took control to see what he could do to change it. He recognized that the workplace had changed, developed a strategy and steered his own career.

Understanding that the workplace has changed and assuming control and responsibility for your career are mandatory requirements in today's world. Robert Schaen, former comptroller of Chicago-based Ameritech, says, "The days of the mammoth corporations are coming to an end. People are going to have to create their own lives, their own careers and their own successes. Some people may go kicking and screaming into the new world, but there is only one message there: You're now in business for yourself."[20]

---

* *Name and some details have been changed.*

PART TWO:

SUCCESS STRATEGIES

3.

MAKING A THOUGHTFUL CAREER MOVE

There are two basic reasons people find themselves making a job or career move—one is it's an option they have chosen; the other is that they were forced to. Oddly enough, while the emotional, financial and practical pressures may be different, there are many similarities in making a voluntary or involuntary move. The similarities lie in *the process you must go through* to make the change, in either situation.

In both circumstances, there are factors you can't control, like when you will find a new job, or who exactly you'll be working for or with, or whether you will have to make a long commute to take the job you really want. If you haven't made a career or job change in a while, the process may seem scarier to you than to someone who has maneuvered through one or more changes.

Likewise, in both situations, there are things you can control—what kinds of opportunities you consider, whether or not you investigate new careers, what kind of goals you set and how much effort you put into your search.

It is important to define what you can and cannot control, and take charge of what you can, turning the process into a "thoughtful move." If your situation was forced upon you, this approach will help minimize the "victim" mentality. If you are making a voluntary change, it will help with the stress you experience as you hold down one job while looking for another. People who view their changed situation as a thoughtful move realize they are now in an evolving process, and come to learn that the psychology of career change, regardless of its origin, is basically the same—scary, interesting, exhilarating and plain tedious all at the same time. And unavoidable. The first thing to do is to identify the immediate tasks that need to be done and get going.

Assessing Your Job Values

A lot of people in the process of change are questioning not only their professions, but core issues, like their *job values*. Forced to stop and evaluate their circumstances, many are finding their values have changed dramatically.

Actually, the questioning of values began before the current dramatic changes in the workplace. American workers in general, and the baby boomers in particular, have been experiencing the "what's-it-all-about syndrome" for some time. In 1975, people felt work was their number-one priority and leisure was necessary to recharge their batteries. But by 1989, a Roper survey of Americans' attitudes showed that more people said that they worked in order to have fulfilling leisure time.[1]

As people find career limits thrust on them, they increasingly question their values. People are deciding that if they can't *have it all*, then they want to pick what they will have. In a survey of American workers aged 25 to 49, 75 percent said they wanted to return to a simpler society with less emphasis on material wealth; 62 percent said a good family life was the most important factor in making them feel successful. Only 10 percent said their career motivation was "earning lots of money." Today's senior and middle managers rank "pay" as the fourth most important job factor, while "having challenging work" is first.[2]

It is critical to identify *what is important to you* and then translate this into the *kinds of changes* you want to make.

Your *criteria* for identifying values and changes will come from:

- Reviewing your past experiences and skills and seeing what you liked and didn't like.

- Taking as objective a look as possible at your industry and/or profession to determine its potential (or lack thereof).

- Thinking about who you are *now* and what the person you are *today* would like to do.

- Considering the responsibilities, obligations and freedoms you have today.

Are You In Sync With Your Company?

Ask yourself if you share enough in common with how your company reacts to its environment and how its employees react in their jobs. For example, when things get hectic at work, do people respond the way you do when you are under pressure? If the answer is "no," you may be in a work environment that is not compatible with the way you work.

Most of Rob Mason's* career has been in marketing. Marketing departments are usually hectic. In his last company, when things got crazy, Rob and his co-workers divided up the problems and worked individually, making lots of phone calls and going to other parts of the company to troubleshoot. He liked this because the high level of activity mirrored the way he personally reacts to crises.

It's different in Rob's current company. When there are problems, everyone writes long memos and has all-day, lunch-brought-in, no-break meetings in the conference room. Rob is going crazy.

In terms of getting things done, Rob's first company didn't necessarily function any more or less efficiently than his second. The difference is that reactions to crises at his first employer matched Rob's style, while reactions at his second employer are opposite his, and therefore uncomfortable.

Has Your Company Changed?

Companies change constantly, in both good and bad times. They reorganize, create new products, get rid of old products and sometimes even change their entire purpose for being in business. They get acquired by others or divide into more than one company. In 1989, only 50 percent of the Fortune 500 companies that existed in 1980 were still around in their original structure.[3]

Whenever companies change, it affects their employees. The effect can be minor or it can completely change their jobs.

Cynthia Graham* was hired by an electronics manufacturer as a customer service representative for a particular product line. Two weeks after she started, the company reorganized and she was reassigned to an entirely different product line. This new line wasn't her area of expertise, it wasn't what she wanted to do and she wasn't very happy about it.

Job situations changed for Cynthia, as they do for many workers today. While your job title may be the same, the situation in which you're working may not. For example:

- You are working with a different product, service or function.

- You have been moved and are working with different people.

- You have a totally different job.

- Your department or boss has lost influence or importance.

- New management has come in. You are now viewed as part of the "old guard" and are politically out of favor.

What these circumstances have in common is that you now find yourself in a different situation. Even if you have the same position, you seem to have a different job and/or seem to be working in a different company. These changes can mean that *your job may no longer be appropriate or suitable for you.*

Do You Have Realistic Expectations About Your Company?

Many companies have "mission statements" or "corporate philosophies" that spell out company beliefs, what the organization stands for, what its values are, how it views its relationship to the community. These statements are developed in good will and generally express positive intentions towards a business' employees, customers and its community. Businesses vary in the emphasis they actually place on corporate beliefs and values. For example, organizations like Nordstrom, Disneyland or Hewlett Packard spend a great deal of effort teaching employees the "Disney way" or the "Nordstrom way." Likewise, equal effort is devoted to publicizing "the way" to customers and the world at large.

But even in the most dominant corporate cultures, your day-to-day work experience is defined by the people you actually work with. In fact, on an individual level, work is really *being a part of a group of people who live with each other every day.* It is no different than being among family and friends. This means there are miscommunications, personality conflicts and mistakes. If you work for the boss-from-hell, your work is defined by this immediate daily reality, rather than your company's formally stated position on employee relations.

Genna Brownwich* was a paralegal, liked her job and was working for a company with a great reputation. However, she was putting in long hours working for a particularly demanding attorney. Her job stress started causing health problems, and her relationship with her husband grew strained. Genna tried a lot of different things. She saw a therapist, as did her husband. She got the human resources representative to mediate between her and her boss. But things did not get better. Genna decided to make a move and eventually found a new position with a more reasonable work schedule. Within a few weeks her health problems disappeared, and her relationship with her husband improved.

The "right" job environment can play a major role in one's general well-being. "There's quite a bit of research that suggests that for people who aren't happy with their jobs or careers, it adversely affects mental health, physical health, satisfaction with life in general," says Michael E. Mills, a professor of psychology at Loyola Marymount University.[4]

If your work situation is troubled, evaluate it as thoroughly as Genna did. Try as hard as she did to see if it can be fixed. But be realistic about your expectations. While you want to work in a comfortable environment with decent people, keep in mind that companies are composed of everyday people who do not put on perfected "work personalities" when they go to work. They usually "come as they are."

Is Your Industry's Culture or Value System Right for You?

Industries, like companies, develop *cultures* or *value systems*. Unlike companies, these systems may not be deliberately created, but instead have evolved over time as a result of common characteristics about the industry and the people in it.

The advertising industry, for example, is generally a hectic one. It is the norm for people in advertising agencies to work long hours, on weekends or even holidays. Those who like this environment are proud of the industry's "work ethic." They even brag to each other about how many hours they put in during a week. A copywriter will say, "Boy, I haven't had a weekend off in three weeks." An account executive will reply, "I haven't had one off in four weeks." It almost becomes a contest.

Whether or not working long hours or adhering to other industry-specific customs is "good" is irrelevant. What is important is whether you like to work this way. If you prefer structured hours and a quiet working environment, then advertising is not a good fit for you. Or, if you are a high-energy person and are in an industry like insurance that "moves slowly," you may get very impatient and frustrated.

Check out your industry to see if its *attitudes, rhythms and pace* mesh with yours. If they do not, you may need to make a change.

Has What You Enjoy Doing Changed?

People say, "I've been in my career for eight (or 10 or 15) years and I don't like it any more. I must have made a mistake." But often, "making a mistake" is not the right conclusion. Rather, people's goals, ambitions and needs may have changed from when they made that first career choice. Often careers aren't chosen, but are "fallen into" instead. Many people take or are promoted into a job in a field unfamiliar to them and stay in this field without ever really consciously choosing it. Down the road, these people may question their careers for the first time and discover that their field is not what they would have proactively chosen.

People who consciously select an occupation do so because it fulfills the needs and aspirations they had when they selected it. While relevant then, these needs and aspirations often change. When this happens, it's time to try something else.

Max Striber* was a successful manufacturing executive for 18 years. He thrived in the consumer products industry and was a master at company politics, quickly advancing from line supervisor to senior vice president of manufacturing for one of his industry's leaders. If anyone had ever told him that he would someday start his own one-person consulting business, he would have laughed at them.

But four years ago, his work stopped being satisfying. He changed jobs, thinking a new company would restore his enthusiasm. It didn't. After much soul-searching, Max recognized that he liked the operations aspect of his job, but felt burdened by the administrative work. He no longer enjoyed the policymaking and employee-management responsibilities, even though he had sought and enjoyed his prominent position.

Max was smart and willing to take a risk. Rather than stay in his position and decide that he must have picked the wrong career path, Max bravely left his company and started his own one-person consulting firm. Using his many contacts, he built a business focusing on providing guidance in the areas of manufacturing, operations and inventory management to companies in his industry. It took some adjusting to change from being a high-profile executive in a large company to a one-man shop, but two years later, Max has renewed enthusiasm for his work and his high energy level is back.

Are You Burned-Out?

Are you burned-out? Do you, or did you:

- Get in late or leave early on a regular basis?

- Hate going to work?

- Call in sick or leave because of illness?

- Feel grumpy and miserable most of the time while at work?

- Often think: *I'm working really hard but I'm not getting things done?*

- Get a lot of criticism or warnings?

- Argue or find yourself in conflict with others?

If you answered "yes" to more than one of these questions, you may be "burned-out." But before you diagnose this as the problem, understand what burn-out is and is not.

Most people equate burn-out with having too much work to do. While a heavy workload can certainly contribute to burn-out, the real factor is how you feel about your work. **"Stress, in and of itself, does not cause burn-out."** Rather, burn-out has been defined as "a gradual erosion of [people's] spirit and zest as a result of the daily struggles and chronic stress that are typical of everyday life and work—too many pressures, conflicts, demands and too few emotional rewards, acknowledgements and successes."[5] Some people function very well in "stressful, demanding careers." But this is because they are in situations where they feel that their work is recognized and has meaning, that their efforts are appreciated. People become burned-out when their jobs are stressful and they do not feel their work makes a difference or that they are appreciated.

Ask yourself: Do you feel in control? Do you feel your work is recognized? Do you feel the results of your job help your organization or your work aspirations?

Realize that different people experience burn-out in different ways. One person may be depressed, another may become argumentative, while a third might become ill.

Jeanne Kramer* performed well in her accounting manager position. Then, corporate finance reporting responsibilities were added to her department at the same time that layoffs were made, leaving Jeanne with almost twice the amount of work and half the staff. She continued to do a great job, even under these circumstances. But she found herself getting very anxious while driving to work and doing odd things, like counting street signs—each sign she saw meant she was closer to work. While Jeanne had never seen "Do you count street signs?" as a question in a job burn-out quiz, she eventually realized that this, as well as her anxiety, was an indication for her that something was wrong.

Some careers intrinsically have a high burn-out rate. Identify whether or not you are in one of them. Care-giving professions such as nursing, social work and teaching are fields where people burn-out a lot—the never-ending chain of people needing help and the problems or pain that these people are experiencing can cause professionals to eventually feel overwhelmed.

Are You Being Realistic About Work?

Are you expecting your job or your work environment to be perfect? Work is no different than life in general; it has its ups and downs. Loving your work is a nice aspiration, but loving it completely is never a realistic one, even in good times. It is like expecting a marriage or relationship to always be perfect. In fact, a good way to evaluate your job is by thinking about it as a relationship. If your job was a friendship or a marriage, how would you say it was doing?

Step back and take an overview of how you feel about your work. Look to see if there is a sense of balance:

- Does what you like outweigh what you dislike?

- During a six-month period, were things all right more than 50 percent of the time?

- Do you like the lifestyle that your work affords?

If your answers to questions like these are affirmative, you probably enjoy your work, despite some dislikes or rough times.

Using Personal Criteria to Decide on the Next Step

Write down what is important to you. Prioritize it. Develop a picture of the kind of change you want to make. Then include your obligations, responsibilities and freedoms—**don't forget the practicalities**. Are you making a high salary that will be difficult to duplicate? Do you have a spouse and three small children whose health care is covered by an excellent policy with your present employer and will be hard to replace? Sometimes, rather than take on a job change, you may decide to stay where you are. Or, if everything is all right, but you don't get charged up every day, look at other ways that you could make your job more interesting.

Remember that different things are important to different people. There is a wide comfort-level spectrum in the work world, and it's important to figure out where you are on this spectrum. It is a matter of weighing the good against the bad and seeing how you come out.

Sylvia Narlin's* ultimate choice was perhaps not one that most people would make, but it was right for her. Sylvia was a statistical analyst and loved her job. As a result of her excellent work, she eventually was rewarded with a move to a managerial position. But for Sylvia, the reward felt more like a punishment. In her new managerial role, she had more people contact, conducted and attended meetings, supervised staff and spent a lot of time on the phone with other departments. But Sylvia just wanted to work with statistics. "I want a job where I spend most of the day on my computer and don't have to deal with all these people," she told an astonished friend. Finally, Sylvia talked to her boss and explained her unhappiness in her new position. While at first surprised, her boss understood Sylvia's viewpoint, though foreign to his own way of thinking, and he agreed to make some changes. Sylvia was able to again focus on statistical work and reduce her contact with people to a level that felt right to her.

It's important to figure out your own situation and act accordingly. If you are unemployed and hated your last job most of the time, you need to focus on new opportunities. If you are employed earning good money but find working for your boss is literally making you sick, you need a new boss, which may entail changing jobs or employers.

Resolving Your Personal Tug of War

Finding where you best fit in the workplace may mean first resolving the tug of war between your values and needs. We need money, but we still want decent lives. Grey Advertising conducted a survey from which it identified a large new demographic group it called the "new grown-ups," accounting for 57 percent of all American households. The people in this group, Grey found, "are placing more value on home, family and friends—but they haven't abandoned the goals of self-fulfillment and career development."[6] This can be a tough balancing act. But it's a proactive move. In your quest to attain a balance between your personal and professional lives, you will be creating new options and discovering new alternatives.

---

* Names and some details have been changed.

4. *L*AYOFF CASUALTIES AND SURVIVORS

I f you've been laid off, it may not provide a lot of comfort to
know you are not alone. Almost two million people lost their
jobs during the recession that began in 1990. Another *375,000
jobs a year* are estimated to be eliminated by layoffs up
through 1997.[1]

The meaning of the term "layoff" itself has changed. It was
originally applied to employees who were asked to leave because of a work shortage, but who could be expected to be
called back when things picked up. But today, the term "laid
off" is virtually synonymous with "permanently terminated."
While unemployment reached double-digit figures at times
in earlier recessions, these high numbers were caused mainly
by *temporary* layoffs, not permanent ones.[2] Total unemployment from the most recent recession may be less than that
of prior recessions (in the 1970s and 1980s), but a larger
proportion, 85 percent, is comprised of workers who have been
permanently let go, as compared to 56 percent in previous
recessions.[3]

There are as many terms used to refer to layoffs as there
are reasons. During the last few years, terms like "rightsizing,"
"reshaping," "re-deploying," "de-selection," "side-lined" and
"benched" have been used by companies in addition to the
good old standbys of "downsizing" and "restructuring." In-

stead of talking about cutbacks, companies speak of "the new reality of doing business" and "operational synergies." They cloak their decision-making in terms like "checking under the hood," "putting the brakes on" or getting down to their "fighting weight."[4]

Whatever it's called, if you've been "rightsized," it probably doesn't feel right to you, and being "de-selected" is pretty hard on the ego and the pocketbook. Instead, you are likely experiencing disbelief, numbness and anger. One unemployed man interviewed in a state unemployment office found it hard to believe he was there. "It seems very unnatural," he said. "[Not like] everything you've ever been taught—that you go to college and work hard and do your job and everything will be hunky-dory. And then the whole world just gets turned upside down."[5]

Working Out the Immediate Logistics
Dealing With Your Employer

Uncomfortable as the situation may be, the first thing to do is deal with the immediate practicalities. This usually means working out the terms of your leaving with your employer.

The termination process is a difficult one for your employer as well as for you. This doesn't mean you have to be sympathetic. Rather, just recognize that everyone involved is tense and uncomfortable, at the very least.

Your employer, of course, has the advantage because people in the company are prepared and know what is going to happen. They often have developed procedures and have held training sessions on the proper way to handle employee terminations.

Current "termination wisdom" suggests that companies conduct layoffs in the most structured, brief and unemotional way possible. There are many guidelines, such as "do it in a neutral site like a conference room or the employee's office so that you can leave," "write a script and rehearse it" and "don't get into arguing about why it is happening, the discussion shouldn't take longer than 10 or 15 minutes." If you are part of a large layoff, you are likely to feel "processed" and that your termination is one tedious, small step in a very big process.[6]

Often, you won't have a lot of say in what the terms of your leaving are. Be aware that companies do not have to offer severance pay, although many of them do. While one to two weeks of pay for each year of employment is an often-used guideline, company policies on severance packages can be enormously different, depending on industry, salary, title and the individual organization's policy.[7] One Philadelphia outplacement firm found that 80 percent of U.S. employers have severance policies for laid-off executives, managers and supervisors. Another study found the average severance package provided three months of pay for engineers; four months for human resources; five months for employees in marketing and sales, accounting, finance operations and information systems; six months for corporate staff and seven months for general management and science professionals.[8]

Policies vary even within companies. Between June 1986 and December 1989, Hughes Aircraft Co. laid off 19,000 employees who, in most cases, received "little more than two weeks' notice and a handshake." In July of 1992, Hughes announced that it would lay off an additional 9,000 employees by the end of 1993. But these employees were eligible for up to 40 weeks of severance pay, six months of health care coverage and $5,000 in retraining aid. Why this dramatic difference? Hughes attributed it to policy changes made to more closely resemble those of companies in the commercial markets that the beleaguered aerospace company hopes to penetrate.[9]

Be aware that other benefits besides *pay* may be part of your severance package. Under the Consolidated Omnibus Budget Reconciliation Act (COBRA), companies with 20 or more employees have to offer health insurance at a group rate for up to 18 months after termination of your employment.[10] The rate is usually significantly higher than what you have been paying, but it does allow you to continue your coverage. Some employers will pay all or part of your COBRA coverage. If they don't offer to, *ask*.

If you have money in a pension plan, work closely with the human resources representative to be sure that you understand your choices in how these funds are disbursed.

Be sure to check into *all* the options offered by your employer. In addition to health insurance, these may include, but are not limited to, outplacement services (job-search counseling and/or services paid for by your employer), retraining funds, as well as facilities, resources and equipment for conducting your job search.

Exploring All the Resources

Look into resources outside your company, too. Find out if you are eligible for unemployment benefits. Never be ashamed to do this—it's there and you have earned it. While you are at your state unemployment office, check to see if it offers a free job-search program, many of them do. Don't stop here. Support-group training and resources may be offered by your community or state. If things are really tight, look into state and federal support options like food stamps. Get whatever help is available, think in terms of survival, don't get caught up in misdirected feelings of pride. *Find out about and take advantage of every kind of help that is available to you.*

Sanity and Relationships

Giving Yourself a Little Understanding

Being laid off is something over which you have no control. As one outplacement counselor puts it, "Your job can be controlled by a board of directors 10,000 miles away who speak a different language."[11]

Experiencing a job loss is like experiencing any other significant loss. Everyone goes through the classic grief cycle: denial, anger, bargaining, depression and acceptance.[12] It's important to realize that everyone has these kinds of feelings, and recognizing them can help you put them behind you and get on with the task of finding a new job.

In a landmark study conducted by Southern Methodist University and outplacement specialists Drake Beam Morin, two groups of executives who had been laid off for six months were tracked. Half of the group was asked to take 20 minutes a day for five days a week and write down their thoughts and emotions about being laid off and its effects. The second group was asked to take the same amount of time, but, instead, to write about the logistics of their job search, such as time management. Three months later, almost one-third of the group that wrote about their feelings had a new job, while all in the second group had yet to be employed. After eight months, over half of the "feelings-writing" group were employed, while only 14 percent of the second group had secured positions. Dr. James Pennebaker, the psychology professor who conducted the study, believes those who wrote about their feelings were better able to get past bitterness and anger and make a decision to move forward in their job search with a positive attitude.[13]

Recognizing Your Identity Crisis

Besides providing economic support, work is usually a big part of a person's life and identity. It's normal to experience the "fish-out-of-water" syndrome. Most of our daily habits are tied around work. When you aren't working, the daily routine changes. ". . . Sunday afternoon you realize that on Monday morning you have no place to go," says an unemployed aerospace engineer.[14] Even small things, like deciding what clothes to wear, can be hard because they are all reminders that things aren't normal. I once worked with a client who said that it was like "not having any mirrors in my life, I couldn't see who I was."

People often find that having no schedule and all the time in the world to look for a job makes it hard to plan. They are used to juggling time and having to sandwich everything into their schedules, from leisure activities to getting to the dry cleaners. Being faced with what can be a very large task— making your next career move—and having no time structures other than "as soon as possible" to plan it around, can be very disorienting. It's easy to end up having "bathrobe days," when you get up planning to make phone calls or finish your résumé, and at four o'clock in the afternoon find yourself staring at the television or thumbing through a magazine.

Interacting With Family, Friends and Business Associates

Don't be surprised if your family and friends "get weird" just when you need them the most. Unfortunately, people aren't comfortable with someone who has lost his or her job. Part of the reason is they feel bad and want to help, but there is usually very little that they can actively do. People don't like feeling helpless. Sometimes they will avoid or be rude to the person that causes them to feel that way, even though these responses are irrational. A common reaction is to blame the person who lost his or her job for the circumstances. The unemployed often receive undeserved explicit or implicit "What did you do wrong to be let go?" messages from those close to them. A 56-year-old hotel architect, laid off by Walt Disney Imagineering, says, "There is a lot of stress to deal with, including family stress. I think my wife initially felt resentment. I think she felt, 'Why can't you bring home the bacon?' "[15] Also, the idea of unemployment pushes everyone's buttons. People can't help thinking, "Gosh, that could be me." It brings up their own insecurities. It makes them uncomfortable and may cause them to distance themselves from you. One unemployed salesperson said, "It's like we've come down with a dreaded disease that just might be contagious."[16]

When the other person is someone emotionally and financially intertwined with you, it's even more difficult. Spouses of either sex are often very frightened and threatened when their mate is out of work. This is true whether or not the spouse works, since two-income households are generally running at two-income spending levels.

If your relationships are getting bumpy, get professional counseling. **Job loss is a well-recognized crisis, and many counselors are experienced in working with spouses, significant others and family members in this situation.** "Losing a job can be as traumatic as a death in the family," says Ruth Mohre, a faculty member at the Ackerman Institute for Family Therapy in New York. "As with any loss, you have to allow your mate to grieve and be upset. . . . [But] the strain isn't any easier on the spouse still employed—and [he or she] too need to vent [his or her] feelings. The trick is to avoid getting bogged down in the venting process so that you can keep moving forward."[17]

Children are a whole other problem. No matter what their age, it's hard to decide what and how much to tell them. Children old enough to understand what is going on can run a gamut of emotions from helpful, to scared, to angry. Your five-year-old may offer up her piggy bank, and your 10-year-old may announce that he won't spend any more money going to the movies. But don't be surprised if the opposite happens. I've had clients whose teen-age sons and daughters have greeted them after a hard day of job hunting with, "Are you ever going to get a job?" or "Does this mean I can't get those shoes?" or "Something's wrong with you, you should have found a new job by now." (Actually, spouses and significant others have been known to pipe up with these kinds of comments too.) Dr. Lee Salk, author and clinical professor of psychiatry and pediatrics, says, "It's fine to admit that you're not happy about the situation—hiding all negative emotions isn't a good lesson either. What you need to avoid is the sense that there's nothing anyone can do. Focusing the family on specific steps each member can take can turn a crisis into a positive and empowering experience."[18] Family trips to the movies, for example, can be changed to afternoon shows which are often cheaper than evening shows. Dance or music lessons can be switched from more costly private instructors to community center classes for the interim. Older children in their teens can even help with job-search tasks, such as verifying the names and addresses of prospective employers or conducting job-hunt research in the local library.

It's hard. Sit down and talk with your family, friends or anyone else you are involved with emotionally and financially. Try to make everyone aware that this is a tense time, and everyone needs to try to be kind to each other. Also, let your family know it's okay to express their fears, and, likewise, give yourself a break and don't hold it all in. Above all, keep in mind that unemployed people and their families and friends get stressed and don't always interact appropriately. It's tricky for everyone to find the right balance between when to comfort, when to ask for comfort, when to express their fears, and when to back off and say nothing.

Don't keep the fact that you are unemployed a secret from business associates; these include peers, customers, vendors and suppliers. It's common to feel embarrassment and shame and attempt to hide the fact that you are not working, but it's how you perceive your current situation and react to it emotionally, not the actual situation, causing these feelings. Remember, some two million others have lost their jobs. People know what is happening; they won't think you are a flake. Actually, you need to let people from your business world know you are out of work because you are going to ask for their help when you mobilize your job search. Even though it may be painful, it's important to preserve these relationships. Don't fade out of sight.

Attitude Does Make a Difference

How you approach your unemployment and subsequent career search will make the difference. A positive attitude can give you the energy to send out 20 letters or, as in the case of the executives who wrote about their feelings, move you faster toward employment. For everyone involved, the path to re-employment will be easier if you view it as a temporary set-back from which you'll recover, as opposed to a permanent debilitating situation.

Survival Techniques for the Layoff Survivor

Even if you haven't been laid off, it's very likely that you work in a company where there have been layoffs. It's nor-mal to worry about job security when you are in a company that has been letting people go. A January 1993 survey by the Associated Press showed that 37 percent of all Ameri-cans are worried that someone in their family will be laid off.[19] In a 1991 survey of employees in 909 firms where layoffs had taken place, 70 percent of the employees who were still work-ing were worried about keeping their jobs.[20] If this was a physical disease, it would be an out-of-control epidemic. In another study, 46 percent of 1,299 respondents indicated that they felt increased pressure on their performance at work to maintain their jobs.[21] "Job insecurity" has been cited as the number-one workplace issue of the 1990s.[22]

Workplace specialists formally recognize these kinds of feelings as "survivor syndrome." People with survivor syn-drome are scared they will lose their jobs. Like Californians who suffer damage in earthquakes or Floridians devastated by hurricanes, many layoff survivors are convinced there will be "another one" and that they might not make it through the next time. Even those with outstanding performance records don't feel that their past history will provide any guar-antee of longevity. And often they are right.

Survivors of layoffs experience grief and anger over the loss of fellow workers. Everyone spends a lot of time with co-workers. Often "work families" are created. The loss of a friend made at work, or of peers—like the two other people that were on your sales team—can be as troubling as the loss of a fam-ily member or outside-of-work friend.

The people who are left after a layoff usually have more work to do. The workload gets redistributed, and those remaining often have new and unfamiliar responsibilities. A study by the American Management Association showed that workers' compensation claims increased in one-third of the companies surveyed where layoffs had taken place. Janet Douglas, a workplace consultant, blames this increase in injuries on the fact that surviving workers are often performing unfamiliar jobs.[23]

On the emotional side, this heavier workload can cause anger and frustration and add to the other negative feelings already there. And like survivors of other disasters who have been studied (such as passengers who walked away from plane crashes), layoff survivors often feel guilty, even though it's irrational. They feel guilt over still having their jobs, over making it through the cutback and remaining employed.

Layoff survivors often end up feeling the same kind of loss of control as those who were actually let go. They get anxious, worry about money and finances, and their self-esteem is affected. They get stressed, perform less well and get sick. Industrial psychologist Karl Kuhnert says, "We've seen the same sort of elevated symptoms of ill health in people who are insecure on the job as in those who have had job losses."[24] But unlike the unemployed, layoff survivors usually don't get much sympathy or counseling because they are considered the "lucky ones"—after all, they are still working. "The attitude," writes Harry Woodward, co-author of *After-Shock: Helping People Through Corporate Change*, "[is that] you should feel fortunate if you have a job, so get with the program."[25]

How to Cope

There is no magic recipe for coping, but there are some things you can do. First, acknowledge your feelings so you can get some perspective on them. Most employers and employees want to ignore their feelings or deny any atmosphere of job insecurity. But this won't make them go away. Face up to the feelings and then you can deal with them.

Don't fall into the trap of trying to be compulsively perfect so you won't be let go. Being perfect is impossible, and trying to achieve perfection can have the opposite effect, making you obsessive, paranoid and miserable, which won't help your job performance. When layoffs occur, "a climate of fear takes hold in which the universal goal is to survive rather than to perform. Fearful of incurring the boss's ire, employees come to work determined to do one thing—stay out of trouble. In this environment, creativity, productivity, quality and service decline," says Jeffrey Davis, managing partner of Mage Centers for Management Development.[26]

Taking Charge

The most important thing that you can do is *take control of your career* and start developing your own job security. Begin by putting your career portfolio together, assess what you've done and what you know, go a step further and put a résumé together. Start thinking about new companies, industries or careers. While it can be hard to find the time, and even harder to motivate yourself, develop a backup plan to help you feel like you have some control.

I live in California and I have an earthquake preparedness kit in the trunk of my car. I've only camped out once in my life, and I would probably be too tense with fright to eat the freeze-dried food in my kit if the "Big One" came while I was on the road, but I do feel better that I have done something to prepare for the possibility. Get your preparedness kit together.

5.

WHAT EMPLOYERS ARE LOOKING FOR

In terms of the workforce, America's organizations are truly between a rock and a hard place. On the one hand, companies have reduced their staffs and have fewer employees. On the other, they need to be more productive, innovative, creative and competitive than at any time in the past. The dilemma is not just to make do with fewer employees, but to understand markets and competition, create and bring new products into the marketplace more quickly than ever before, profoundly strengthen customer service and take full advantage of all the benefits that technology has to offer. To meet the challenge, organizations need to learn to function with fewer people, and they need these people to be more educated, productive and creative than any workforce in the past.

With fewer jobs and more people looking for work, competition can be tough as new work-force entrants, experienced mid-careerists and older workers all compete in the same job pool, and sometimes for the same positions. The number of job seekers is expected to increase dramatically by the year 2000, when virtually half of the workforce will be composed of baby boomers.[1] Even without current cutbacks, this glut of baby boomers, alone, would create a shortage of opportunities.

For those who do find work, climbing up the corporate ladder has become trickier today than it used to be. The ladder is shorter by a number of rungs. In the past, large organizations averaged 10 to 15 levels of employees, and a successful employee could expect to be promoted six, seven or perhaps even 10 times within that company. Now with "flatter" organizations and far fewer levels of management, there are fewer opportunities for promotion.[2] And guided by newly found caution, companies are promoting more slowly when they do promote. In the early 1960s and 1970s, corporate fast-trackers averaged promotions every 18 to 24 months. But by 1990, this timespan had stretched to a minimum of 36 to 48 months.[3]

Why People Get Hired or Promoted

The same traits and circumstances that get people hired also get them promoted. Entry or advancement can often mean being the right person in the right place at the right time. There are two important variables at work in the hiring and promotion process. The first is *you as a product:* your personality, actual experience, abilities, education and training. The second is *timing or circumstances:* who else is being considered for the position, what kind of person an employer thinks is best, how well you potentially fit into the organization and every other element of chance. In a promotion, relevant circumstances might include: your exposure within the organization, others who are qualified, whether or not your current boss wants to hang on to you and a myriad of other possibilities that can make up work situations.

It's critical to recognize the existence of both the "you as a product" and the "circumstances" factors. How much each weighs in a particular situation depends on the elements that make it up. Some circumstances can be controlled or, at best, influenced; others cannot, and it's important to recognize which are which.

While circumstances may be beyond your reach, you do have control over how you present yourself as a product in the workplace. With the goal of maintaining and achieving high productivity, employers are seeking out employees who are proactive, as opposed to passive. Thus, as a "product" in the workplace, the key attributes in demand are:

- Your knowledge and ability to learn.
- Your decision-making skills.
- Your flexibility, adaptability and initiative.
- Your communication and teamwork skills.

The Knowledge Attraction

First in importance is being "knowledgeable." Organizational expert Peter Drucker says, ". . . in this society, knowledge is *the* primary resource for individuals and for the economy overall."[4] At the very least being knowledgeable means having good basic reading, writing and mathematical skills. But in most jobs, it goes beyond these basics to include the ability to conceptualize, plan, understand and interpret data. And in virtually any job, it's essential to be "computer literate," often a misunderstood term. Computer literacy doesn't mean you have to understand how computers work, but rather that you know how to use them to get your particular job done. For example, at Mrs. Fields Cookies, one of the biggest cookie retailers, store employees can key into a daily planning program and enter local conditions such as "the schools are closed today." The program analyzes past history, current trends and guidelines, and presents a production plan showing what should be produced for this particular day and who is expected to buy it.[5] But to do this, the same people who bake and sell the cookies also need to be able to operate this computer system.

Knowledge should no longer be limited to one area of expertise. Don't be a "totalist" with all of your knowledge eggs in one basket.[6] It is very likely that you will "wear more than one hat" in any position and that your expertise will span both technical *and* general areas, such as communication or management. Pat Gelsinger, an engineer with Intel, cites the growing need for "renaissance engineers," people who have a good business sense in addition to strong technical abilities.[7]

The breadth-of-knowledge requirement applies to all industries. In addition to knowing their product lines, salespeople often need to have enough computer knowledge to place their orders, juggle inventories and troubleshoot shipping and delivery problems. Specialists are suddenly finding it necessary to step back and look at the big picture. "My job is a lot harder now," says a business agent for a local union. "I used to fight for shift discipline, pension benefits. That was easy. Now I have to sit down and figure out how to drive overhead costs out of the business to come up with a competitive bid."[8]

Since you will need to become knowledgeable in many areas, the *ability to learn* is, therefore, a must. Learning, says Charles Handy in *The Age of Unreason*, is not limited to intellectuals.[9] Because technologies and organizations are changing quickly, almost everyone in the workforce will go through periods of having to learn new things and perform new tasks throughout his or her career. The Japanese call this continuous need for self-improvement "kaizen."[10] Everyone needs to practice *kaizen*, from senior executives who must understand and use new computerized data, to administrative assistants who find themselves coordinating complex projects involving several departments, to teachers needing bilingual skills in order to teach their culturally diverse classrooms.

Decision-Making Skills

Being knowledgeable also means being able to solve problems and make decisions. Improved and expanded information technology is allowing companies to put decision-making in the hands of the people actually doing the work. In the past, the role of management was often to collect and understand data and then make decisions and set priorities based on this data. This is changing. Today you are much more likely to make decisions, regardless of your level in an organization, because you will have the information you need to do so.

At Frito-Lay, for example, the role of many employees has drastically changed. As part of its response to heavy competition, the company completely restructured manufacturing processes and brought decision-making down to the employee level on the factory floor. In addition to their technical manufacturing knowledge, employees are trained in business fundamentals, focusing on what consumers want, how to calculate profit and loss, how to improve quality and how each manufacturing plant fits into the company as a whole.

Frito-Lay line workers now enter essential data, like the number of pounds of raw materials being used, such as corn or packaging material, the length of time the assembly line was down for repair or how many man-hours were logged. The computer gives instantaneous feedback on the line's performance, and employees make the next set of decisions based on this feedback. Employees have become much more involved, are taking pride in their work, and profits and market share are up.[11]

Flexibility, Adaptability and Initiative

The workplace changes of the early 1990s are not a one-time phenomenon. Companies will continue to change on an ongoing basis. "The new view is the organization as a kaleidoscope—always changing, always trying to adapt to a continuously changing world," says Steven Kerr, a management professor at the University of Southern California who consults to General Electric.[12]

If organizations are going to keep changing, so must people. *Flexibility, adaptability and initiative* are important traits—if you don't have them, you need to develop them.

Everything is evolving in the workplace—technologies, markets, customers, competition, products. Organizations are

evolving just as quickly. Changes can include almost anything, from how companies develop a new product and get it
to market, to how they automate a manufacturing process or
reorganize a division of the company. To accomplish this transition, companies must have employees who deal effectively
with change. The person who reacts with, "That's not the way
we do it here," may receive an invitation to go elsewhere. Today, even the "CEO can no longer run a company based on
the way things were done when he was down the ranks 20
years ago," says Scott H. Schlecter of L/E/K Partnership, a
consulting firm.[13]

**People must not only recognize the need for change,
accept it and adapt to it, they must go a step further and
initiate it when appropriate.** If, for example, you see a new
use for the product your company makes, tell somebody. If
it's picked up, try to be a part of the team making it happen.
If you figure out a more efficient way to get something done,
bring it to someone's attention. Increasing revenues or re-
ducing costs can enhance your worth.

Communication and Teamwork

Being able to *communicate* is essential. This means really
being able to grasp what you hear and share what you know
so it is fully understood. It goes beyond the garden-variety
"good communication skills" (a catchy phrase put in most
résumés) or simply remembering to tell people to "have a nice
day." In today's workplace, most jobs will involve interacting
with others, and many will involve being part of a team. This
means that you need to be able to speak and write clearly
and to listen carefully. You must be tactful and cooperative,
know how to gain cooperation and be persuasive, yet able to
compromise. In the engineering field, it's called—"concurrent
engineering"—the ability to do your engineering work *and*
communicate about it. "It's not enough to be good technically, you have to be articulate to be in my group," says Helen
Connon, a chemist with Du Pont.[14]

Teamwork is an important concept in the new work-

place, and one that goes beyond being a buzzword that looks good on a résumé, or a concept given lip service in a corporate mission statement. Michael Halloran, national director of executive compensation for Wyatt Co., a human resources consulting firm, puts it this way: "You've got to be more flexible, more able to work with other people in a cooperative way. You've got to remember you are no longer fighting it out."[15]

Many companies are reorganizing their staffs into teams to get products into the marketplace faster. When a team is formed, people from different areas often work together so that several processes can happen simultaneously, as opposed to sequentially. American car manufacturers, for example, are copying Honda Motors' concept of "platform teams" to get cars out faster into the marketplace. Platform teams are typically composed of designers, manufacturing engineers, marketing staff, accountants and line foremen who work together from the concept of a product to putting a customer service system in place.[16] The team movement is extending to small companies as well. At Techmetals, an 80-employee manufacturer in Ohio, teams handle scheduling, delivery and plant layout. Lee Watson, director of improvements, says, ". . . [teams have] simply made us a more efficient company, with better working conditions and a more educated workforce."[17] To work on a team like this—which can exist in virtually any industry—you must not only be able to perform in your area of expertise, but also communicate with others on your team, understand what *they* are doing and work effectively as part of the group to get the job done.

Up-To-Date Management Skills

If the workplace is changing, and workers are changing, then people in management must change too since what makes a good manager is a reflection of what makes any good employee. Managers must learn to manage in a new way— bully bosses are out.[18] Rather than simply telling people what to do, management's role is shifting to motivating, facilitating and guiding employees. Terms used to describe today's managers include "enabler," "coordinator"[19] and "coach."[20]

Managers in the new workplace must lead teams, serve as technical specialists in helping groups and individuals implement new technology, solve problems and promote decision-making and consensus among diverse employees.[21] They also have to inspire employees by helping them understand the company's vision and how to lock into it. This can require some adjustment on the part of managers. "To be open to ideas from anywhere and empower people isn't easy at first if you've been accustomed to another way of doing business," says Jack Welch, CEO of General Electric.[22]

About Promotion

There is no one proven formula for getting promoted, as the Center for Creative Leadership, in Greensboro, North Carolina, found out. The Center studied 66 managers, their bosses, and their bosses' bosses at three Fortune 500 companies, and found a tremendous diversity in why promotions were given and to whom they were given. Promotions weren't always awarded for past performance and there wasn't one single career path that led to them. While performance mattered, some people got promoted because they were available —they were in the right place at the right time. There might have been someone else better qualified, but they weren't deemed as available. Some managers moved up as a result of restructurings, joint ventures or other people's retirement. Others, in fact 35 percent, had "developmental" promotions —they were promoted because of "promise" or perceived potential, rather than performance history. In the study, visibility within the organization emerged as a key factor, and not just in the sense of "who you know." While *who you actually know* is important, *who knows of you* can be equally or even more important. For example, even if some managers in the Center's study didn't directly know the key decision-makers in their organization, their reputations were *known by* these decision-makers as a result of their accomplishments.[23]

In the past, traditional promotion criteria has been based on specific personality traits and performance. *Longevity* and *seniority* counted for a lot; long tenure typically brought promotions, perks and respect. Qualities like *loyalty* and *endurance* were important. Organizations rewarded these traits with upward career movement. And *who you knew* was a big factor, since knowing or not knowing the right people could advance or stall your career.

While these may all still play a role in today's promotion process, often they become almost side issues. **Of greater importance are the same key elements that help people get hired: on the job you must demonstrate and practice a willingness to learn, be knowledgeable, be flexible and creative, take initiative and communicate effectively.**

In addition to understanding the performance criteria for promotion, you need to be savvy about "corporate politics." This means tuning in to office dynamics while avoiding over-involvement. Some people are so involved in workplace politics, they don't focus on their jobs. Others, disdaining the term and what it implies, say, "I don't involve myself in corporate politics, it's demeaning. I'm here to get the job done." Between these two extremes is reality. It is foolish to deny the existence of corporate politics. In any situation, when two or more people are together in an environment there is inter-action. People respond to each other, form judgments and discuss one another. They like some people and don't like others. They compete. All of this is normal human behavior. In the workplace, it just happens to be called "corporate politics." To ignore it, then, is to ignore human interaction and its effects. This is like wearing blinders. Blinding yourself can put you at a disadvantage. If you can only see part of something, you can't evaluate it and make as good a decision as you might if you could see it all.

This doesn't mean you have to go the opposite route and feed the gossip mill or maneuver people around for the sake of maneuvering. Rather, it means you should keep your eyes and ears open, pay attention, and incorporate the information you get into your behavior and decisions. If, for example, you are the protégé of someone nobody likes, you may want to figure out a way of getting a different mentor or downplaying your relationship with your current one if you can do so tactfully. If you work for someone who is a shining star, make it known you are part of the "A Team." Sometimes difficult decisions are involved. If you are offered a job that your best friend at work thought he or she was going to get, your friendship will be strained. On the other hand, not taking the position could send an "I-don't-care-about-getting-ahead" message to your employer and become career suicide if you do want to advance.

Getting on the "Lateral Track"

A new kind of promotion—*the lateral track*—has emerged as organizations have grown flatter. You are on the lateral track when you are given the opportunity to switch departments and assignments, causing you to move laterally *around* the organization rather than upward. Lateral moves are made into different areas, such as marketing, finance, production or research and development.

The lateral track can have tremendous advantages. It results in *cross-training* that lets you gain a breadth of knowledge and experience that will either eventually help move you upward in your current organization or be utilized in another work role.

In the past, lateral moves were sometimes viewed as career bombs and were seen as the equivalent of being "kicked upstairs." This has changed. Instead, the lateral track is a way of grooming employees for eventual "vertical" promotion, retaining good employees when there are no upward opportunities and injecting new perspective and input into the organization. "There are different kinds of opportunities today," says Mona Theobold, manager of sales planning and support in the CAT-scan division of GE Medical Systems in Milwaukee. "You may not be moving up the corporate ladder every year, but you're expanding your knowledge base. I've taken on more and more responsibility and become much more interactive with my colleagues and customers."[24]

Companies are beginning to revamp their salary plans to motivate employees to make lateral moves. RJR Nabisco Food Group, for example, has restructured its salary plan to give pay raises to sideways movers. Corning, Inc. has an incentive program which offers a five-percent increase to managers who make lateral moves.[25] Some large companies, like General Electric, are restructuring job and pay classifications into "broad bands" instead of small incremental hierarchies. A company that, in the past, divided a range of positions among 20 salary classifications, for example, will now collapse all 20 into five "broad-band" classifications. This allows companies to give employees a raise when they are moved laterally without having to give them an upward promotion. A manager, for example, could be classified as a Level 4 for his or her entire career, but the salary range for this level could be from $50,000 to $100,000, allowing for financial raises without a promotion. Broad-banding allows employees to change areas of responsibility and salaries without being controlled by rigid hierarchical position and salary systems.[26]

Managing Your Advancement

Most importantly, try to "do the right thing" for yourself in your organization, focusing on moves that are advantageous to getting ahead and avoiding those that won't help or can even hurt. For example:

• **Be visible.** This doesn't mean you have to know everyone important to your career. Rather, try to be "well-known" through specific goals you have attained, track records you have set, or even particular projects you have managed or presentations you have given. You don't have to be a screaming extrovert or a "pushy person." If your accomplishments are of the caliber to be talked about, they will generate your publicity for you.

- **Be vital and accountable.** If you can, try to work in an area that contributes directly to the bottom line or is measurable in some way. If your results are measurable, it's easier to see your contribution to the company. And if you are involved in the key processes that focus around producing products and marketing them to customers, you're more vital to the organization. If you are an accountant, for example, you might have more chances for promotion in a company whose business is accounting, than in a company producing medical equipment that has a department providing accounting as a support function.

- **Pay attention.** You have to carefully *identify* and *target* upward opportunities, *perform* well and *compete for them.* Today's workplace is no place to be shy and inattentive. You must "know when to hold 'em, know when to fold 'em" sang Kenny Rogers in *The Gambler.*[27] This means recognizing when there are no upward opportunities, or when you are not in the running for them, and deciding on your course of action (which might be staying in your job or looking for a new one, depending on your personal situation). Conversely, it also means being alert to unexpected or sudden opportunities, mobilizing yourself and *going for it* when they do pop up.

- **Don't get too comfortable.** Sometimes people feel very secure in their jobs. They know how to do what they do, and this provides a level of comfort and satisfaction. This is great if you want to stay in your current job, but not so good if you want to get ahead. If you prefer advancement, don't let complacency keep you from doing the right things to progress.

- **Don't let fear stop you.** "Fear is the mind-killer," wrote Frank Herbert in *Dune.*[28] Often, people are afraid to move into the unfamiliar and take the next step forward. It's important not to let this happen. *Remember that everyone does something for the first time.* Most of the time, employees are promoted because of their ability to learn, not their experience. Even if right now you don't know how to do the next job up, you will figure it out when you get there. That's how most of the world works anyway.

Taking Control of Your Own Career

Whether you are trying to get promoted or seeking opportunities with new employers, take control of your career as much as you can. Look at yourself as a marketable product that needs to be current, well-presented and promoted as positively as possible.

How EMPLOYERS ARE PAYING

T o successfully negotiate a salary for a new position or a raise for an existing one, you need to understand how both have been affected by today's changed workplace.

Salaries and Raises in the New Work World

Salaries are not rising as consistently as they have in the past. In fact, in some industries they have dropped, in others they have stagnated and in those where salaries have continued to increase, the rate has been slower than in the past. Raises are reflecting the same trends, with fewer, slower and smaller raises being given.

Workers can no longer count on steady raises. According to the U.S. Department of Labor, the *average* salary increase in 1992 was 2.7 percent.[1] A survey of senior executives in 1,000 large and mid-size companies in more than 40 industries showed 1993 base pay increases at an average of 5.3 percent for senior-level executives and 4.9 percent for middle- and lower-level managers.[2] These figures are quite a drop from 1982, when raises for *all levels* of workers averaged 9.1 percent.[3]

Part of the reason for the decrease and slow-up, especially in the short-term, has been the need for American companies to cut expenses. Lower salaries and raises help reduce costs. Hiring people at lower wages is easier for companies now because there are so many people willing to accept smaller salaries. The average high-level executive starting salary, $140,000 in 1989, was $118,000 in late 1992. Even the wages of workers with college degrees failed to keep pace with inflation, dropping an average of 3.1 percent between 1987 and 1992.[4]

A Change in How People Are Paid

Beyond the current lowering of wages, the nature of employee compensation itself is undergoing fundamental change. Employers are linking pay directly to performance rather than basing it on formally defined job descriptions. Harvard professor Rosabeth Moss Kanter calls this being paid for "performance instead of position" and "contribution instead of status."[5] This fundamental change will have long-term effects, regardless of whether or not wages bounce back from the 1990-1991 recession.

In the past, most employee pay was based on a job structuring system called the Hay Plan, which was established in the 1950s by the Hay Group,[6] a human resources consulting firm. Under this system, and other similar "point-factor" systems, jobs were rated according to the knowledge and problem-solving skills required to perform them, and the position's accountability and magnitude of responsibility. Important criteria, for example, would be how large a manager's staff was, or whether the manager had budget responsibility and, if so, the size of the budget. Lower-level positions were defined in similar ways in terms of scope of activities performed and the knowledge required to do them. Based on all factors in a job, a number of points would be assigned to a position, and this number determined the pay range for that position within the company.

This system worked pretty well in organizations as long as they were stable, even-paced and part of equally stable environments, but became unwieldy as the workplace changed. Today, companies need to be able to react quickly to shifting environments that include new competition and evolving technologies. Products must be brought to the marketplace more quickly and adapted rapidly to changing marketplace demands. Now, organizations are flatter, with fewer layers of management, with decision-making pushed down into non-management levels. Emphasis is being placed on teamwork, customer service and quality.

In response to this evolution, employee compensation plans are being restructured to reflect these changes in productivity, decision-making, teamwork and superior customer service and quality. Mechanics at Pep Boys, for example, are paid with a percentage of the labor charges from the job they do. But unlike others in their industry, they do not receive a percentage of the cost of new parts and materials. In fact, if the job has to be done over, they may lose their percentage of the labor charges. This change in pay has helped curb the overcharging and unnecessary repairs that are common in the auto service business. It has benefited the company, with sales doubling to over $1.1 billion since 1986.[7]

The old methods of evaluating jobs and structuring pay do not fit the new workplace. Ira Kay, managing director for executive compensation at the Hay Group, recognizes that as the goals of organizations change, the system for evaluating jobs must evolve to incorporate these changes.[8] Or as Towers Perrin compensation specialist Christopher Cardwell puts it, "It no longer makes sense to pay people according to the size of their empire."[9]

Pay for Performance

Pay linked to performance, actually, is not a new idea. "Bonuses" have long been a part of management compensation and, in some cases, non-management employee compensation. Usually, however, bonuses were tied to how the company or division did as a whole, rather than an individual's performance. An employee in the accounting department of a manufacturing company could do a great job implementing a new computer system that, in fact, cut costs, but receive no bonus if the manufacturer as a whole didn't meet its goals. Likewise, an indifferent manager and a line worker who barely met production standards could be well rewarded if their company did well, despite their own lackluster performances.

Unlike bonuses, performance pay is a plus for workers, since it links compensation to criteria and measurements individual employees can more directly control or influence, rather than to nebulous overall corporate results. Currently, over 50 percent of the largest businesses in America have performance-based incentive plans, up from 33 percent in 1985.[10]

All levels of employees can be included in these kinds of compensation systems, from line workers to managers. Even board of director compensation is being affected. Some companies, like American Express, increase board meeting participation (often a problem) by deducting money from members' annual retainers if they miss too many meetings. Others, like Whirlpool, are granting stock options to board members if the company's financial performance improves in some measurable way, like annual return on equity. Companies feel that paying directors to do a good job more closely aligns them to the company and its philosophy.[11]

Ways to Pay

The five most common pay-for-performance systems are: profit-sharing, gain-sharing, performance-bonus pay, pay for skill (or knowledge) and entrepreneurial compensation.[12]

Profit-sharing is when employees receive some fractional portion of net profits based on a defined time period during which certain levels of profitability were met. This pay can be immediate or deferred. Profit-sharing plans can include all employees in a company or be limited to just some of them, but seem to be most effective when all employees are included. A survey of 172 large employers showed that 67 percent of the companies that included all employees in their pay-for-performance plan reported significant gains in productivity and improved morale. But among companies whose plans were limited to high-level management, only 40 percent could report comparable improved results.[13]

Gain-sharing is a form of profit-sharing that is based on team performance rather than individual performance. In a gain-sharing system, the contribution that a team of workers can potentially make is defined and calculated. Team contributions can be based on achieving productivity levels, cutting costs and/or other measurable objectives. Team members receive extra pay if their contribution goals are met. The most well-known gain-sharing system is at General Motors' Saturn automotive plant in Tennessee. Successfully negotiated with the United Automobile Workers union, workers' set salaries are about 80 percent of what union members generally get.[14] Workers are paid productivity bonuses in addition to their salary when they meet productivity goals. Gain-sharing can be very profitable for employees, says Jerry Ledford of University of Southern California's Center for Effective Management. "It's not uncommon for successful plans to pay out 20 to 30 percent of base pays."[15]

Another compensation alternative, **performance-bonus pay**, gives employees extra money when they individually meet specific production criteria. The most common examples of performance-bonus pay are commissions and bonuses paid to sales staff meeting individual performance goals.

Then there's **pay for skill**, also known as **pay for knowledge**, which compensates employees when they formally train in new technologies or job skills. Workers are paid for their newly acquired skills regardless of whether or not they actually are used immediately by the employee. Skills can include learning new areas or all of a process of which the employee currently only performs a part. By picking up new skills, for example, some non-management personnel at nine of Corning's 22 companies can raise their base pay from $9.60 an hour to $13.50 an hour. At American Steel and Wire, workers can increase their pay by up to $12,480 by learning as many as 10 new skill areas. Pay-for-skill systems also benefit the company itself. In a study of 27 companies using this system, 70 to 88 percent reported higher job satisfaction, product quality or productivity. Seventy to 75 percent said employee turnover and operating costs had dropped.[16]

A fifth method of pay for performance is based on **employee-generated entrepreneurial ventures**. In this scenario, employees who have ideas for new businesses related to the company start the "businesses" within the company, as opposed to going outside to start their own company. These employees are paid more like "owners" of the business, rather than according to the normal employee pay structure. For example, in addition to a base salary, they are given equity in the "new" company or receive royalties. Of course, if the venture isn't successful, the additional part of the compensation is at risk. Working out the complexities of this kind of system is difficult, and the concept is controversial, but American companies are very interested in exploring it as a way to develop and retain new products and services.

The Good and The Bad

The biggest advantage of employee pay-for-performance systems is that people can have an effect on how much they earn. They may be compensated along with others by achieving the goal criteria of the company's profit-sharing systems or more directly through a pay-for-knowledge system. The other major advantage is that many employees can earn more than they would under older, traditional pay systems.

Employees compensated under these new systems must plan their personal finances accordingly, since, with performance pay, less of an employee's salary is "guaranteed" as part of base pay. Further, base salaries are not being compounded as they have been in the past, and "lump-sum" bonuses, based on the pay-for-performance criteria selected, are not added to employee base salaries. Under the old system, if employees earned $30,000 and got a 9-percent raise, their base pay *now became* $32,700. Under the new systems, employees might earn $30,000 and receive $2,700 or even more in a bonus payment, but their base pay would *remain* at $30,000, and their bonus would not automatically boost next year's compensation.

Thus, compensation can vary from year to year or even month to month, depending on whether criteria are met. When a company has a good year, for example, generous bonuses may be had by all. But in a lean, tough year, pay-for-performance-based pay will be down, lowering overall wages. This variability in compensation is not something most workers are accustomed to, except perhaps for salespeople or senior management. But pay-for-performance compensation is a trend that is probably here to stay. A 1992 study of 1,006 employers showed that 61 percent had pay-for-performance programs, up 10 percent in just one year.[17]

The Impact on Salary Increases

Pay-for-performance systems are having a big impact on raises, as well as initial salaries. Most pay-for-performance plans give employees a lump-sum "bonus" annually or more often. (The exception to this can be pay-for-skill systems, where hourly wages may be increased.) Because this lump payment, contingent on performance, is taking the place of annual raises, the traditional annual merit pay increase is disappearing. In some organizations, base pay raises are being given every two years or even longer, as opposed to yearly. In others, they are being eliminated and replaced by pay-for-performance incentives. This is happening at all employee levels, not just senior management. Even unions are sanctioning this system. One-time bonus payments, in lieu of pay increases, are being incorporated into almost 20 percent of all union contracts, with the exception of the construction industry.[18]

Compensation Expectations

When negotiating a salary or raise, it used to help if you had a sense of "where you were" in your career. If you were in your early twenties, for example, you would focus more on opportunity than salary, looking at the early years as the building blocks of your career. In your thirties and forties, the heat would be on to hike up your pay as much as you could. By your middle or late forties and fifties, your increases would probably slow down, and you would be less inclined to make a move for a moderate increase. Although, if you were really good and found yourself dead-ended, you would want to look at moving to another company, rather than accepting the "bad-news blues" from your employer.

While these overall guidelines are still valid, you should be aware that in today's mercurial workplace, the "appropriateness" of how much someone "should" be making at different career stages has changed substantially. A 29-year-old chemical engineer, for example, may be very well paid, because such people are in demand. But a 42-year-old public school teacher may go through several stagnant years with no salary increases and perhaps even one or more pay cuts. And a 50-year-old manager may be willing to change companies for the same amount of money just to stay employed. When you negotiate for a salary or raise, keep in mind that the traditional career profile has changed. Be realistic and focus on your own circumstances, not on what they were "supposed" to be in yesterday's workplace.

Keeping Current on Salary Trends

Salary ranges vary dramatically by industry, geographic location and level of position. It helps to visit the library and check the most current information before negotiating a salary or raise. Numerous salary surveys are compiled and published.

• Some are put out by magazines and trade publications. *Forbes, Fortune, BusinessWeek,* and *Working Woman* all publish annual salary surveys. The *National Business Employment Weekly,* by Dow Jones, Inc., publishes one which includes cost-of-living comparisons by area and the results of specific occupation salary surveys. *ADWEEK,* a trade publication, prints an annual survey of advertising and marketing salaries. Electrical engineering positions can be found in *Electrical Engineering Times* and *EDN News.*

• Salary surveys are produced by professional and trade associations as well. Look in the *Encyclopedia of Associations* (Gale Research Inc.) or the *National Trade and Professional Associations of the United States* (Columbia Books, Inc.) for the names of over 3,000 associations, many of whom publish salary information.

• Recruiting companies and career experts also produce salary information. Crandall and Associates in New York, for example, puts out an annual survey on salaries in the direct marketing field. Robert Half and Accountemps publish comprehensive salary guides.

• Other sources found at the library include: *The American Almanac of Jobs and Salaries*, the *Professional Careers Sourcebook* and the *American Salaries and Wages Survey.*

• Phone calls or mail inquiries for salary information can be made to the U.S. Bureau of Labor Statistics and government publications like the *Monthly Labor Review*, the *Occupation Outlook Quarterly* or *Compensation and Working Conditions.*[19]

• Don't overlook local resources like your Chamber of Commerce or other local business associations. And sometimes you can get an amazing amount of information by picking up the phone and calling specific businesses. Federal and state laws often mandate the public posting of salary ranges for certain positions. Some companies will include salary information on their telephone job "hot lines."

Perks Besides Money

When negotiating salary and raises, be sure you inquire about options other than salary. There are many other "perks" that may be available. As companies continue to cut costs, alternative forms of compensation are becoming more popular as a way to augment salaries and raises. KPMG Peat

Marwick is offering **appreciation services**, like dry cleaning pickup at the office and free weekend baby-sitting during tax season, to soften the impact of fewer and reduced raises.[20]

In a more traditional mode, many companies are giving **financial incentives** that were formerly limited to senior management levels. Pepsico, Waste Management and Merck are granting stock options to all their full-time employees, regardless of rank.[21] Another popular form of financial incentive is the 401(k) plan, which allows employees to tax shelter a percentage of their earnings and provides some amount of matching funds from the employer after a specified period of time.

Health insurance is obviously an important benefit and perhaps the most controversial one in the United States right now. America's health insurance system is in for some dramatic change over the next several years. During the process, it can be a tough issue for employees. As early as 1990, only 57 percent of the country's workers were able to get health care coverage through their employers, down from 59 percent in 1988. [22]

Vacation time is becoming a perk in a new way. In some companies, vacation time can be "bought" or "sold." Employees at Southern California Edison, for example, can "buy" an extra week of vacation. (This means they can take a week off without pay.) Buying vacation time is very popular at many companies, including Dominion Resources, Education Testing Services and the Carlson Companies. "Selling" vacation time means forgoing vacation and getting pay instead. While not as widely chosen as buying vacation time, it is still a popular option. In a 1992 study of 1,106 companies, 19 percent offered vacation "buy" options, and 18 percent offered "sell" options.[23] The reason behind the popularity of these plans is that people like the flexibility. They have a sense of control over their pay and time, rather than relegating it to company policy.

Another new benefit being offered by companies is **legal services**. AT&T, for example, has a legal insurance plan available to its 450,000 managers. The plan works similarly to health insurance. By taking advantage of group rates, employees have access to a lawyer at a fixed price. While mostly limited to larger companies, some sort of employer-sponsored legal services plan is currently provided to 7.4 million American workers.[24]

Sometimes workers can negotiate for **personalized benefits** that are individualized and attractive to them for specific reasons. Some employees, for example, find that being able to alter their schedule is more important than salary. A human resources manager in a company in New York says, "I know many people who would rather come in to work at 9:30 everyday and not get a raise."[25]

Other options can include career development assistance, like getting your company to pay for a seminar or series of courses, or even image consulting so that you can learn to look more professional. Companies may be willing to spring for health-related options. People have negotiated for fitness program memberships, annual physicals or having the fees paid for joining SmokEnders or Weight Watchers.[26]

Sometimes you can negotiate for a benefit which is particularly useful for you, like parking expenses, short-term loans or membership fees to professional organizations.

Being Reasonable and Realistic

When evaluating salaries and raises, strive to reach a balance between ambition, need and reality. **The most important thought to keep in mind is that, today, companies want to pay you for what you can actually do, and they want to see you do it.** Your abilities and accomplishments are the currencies *you* have to barter in exchange for monetary compensation. "Employers used to pay today's dollar for potential, for tomorrow's dreams," says Andrew Sherwood, chairman of Goodrich & Sherwood, a human resources consulting firm. "Now they pay today's dollars for yesterday's performance."[27]

7.

EDUCATION, TRAINING AND WORK

A Little History About Work and the Education It Requires

In the past, the majority of jobs had to do with making things; they were manufacturing-oriented. Up until the beginning of the 20th century, a worker often performed *all* of the processes necessary to produce a product. This meant that there were "master craftsmen," highly skilled people, like metal workers and carpenters, who developed strong, individual talents and abilities.

When assembly-line manufacturing was introduced, first in the auto industry in the early 1900s, the nature of work changed. Labor was deliberately "de-skilled" as production was broken down into many small, relatively easy-to-do, repetitive tasks. Usually these tasks also involved the use of machinery, which, simply by its nature, eliminated decision-making or personal judgment requirements from the process. Assembly-line workers only needed to know their particular part of a total manufacturing process, as opposed to craftsmen who performed the entire process.

Assembly-line production led to America's high productivity and allowed line workers (many of whom were ultimately unionized) to earn high wages. It also allowed most workers to get by with minimal formal education (usually the equivalent of an eighth-grade education) and still perform their jobs well. The small segment of the population that was college educated easily provided enough people to fill managerial and technical positions requiring more education.

In the 1970s, things began to change. "Low-skill" jobs started to disappear and almost three million manufacturing positions were lost by 1979.[1] By the late 1980s, these changes hit full force as the assembly-line, de-skilled type of labor that led to America's manufacturing success was made obsolete. Gradually, advances in information technology gave workers—who were accustomed to working in "de-skilled" job environments—the opportunity, if not responsibility, to make what had previously been management-type decisions. In fact, when we Americans looked up in surprise at our suddenly strong foreign competitors, we found they had already begun giving workers decision-making power. Production decisions like ordering raw materials, planning inventory and quality control were being placed in the hands of the front-line workers. Work was becoming more complex and "thinking" was emerging as a critical component of many jobs.

The Educational Profile of Today's Workplace

Today's new workplace demands that virtually everyone *think* as part of his or her job. While in the early 1990s, only 22 percent of the jobs in the American workplace needed to be held by people with college degrees, it is expected that *89 percent of all jobs will require cerebral skills by the year 2000*, placing greater emphasis on post-secondary education.[2]

There are differing projections as to how many jobs in the workforce will require advanced education and how much advanced education will be needed. The U.S. Department of Labor says that *almost all* jobs will require at least *one year* of college training. Other workplace experts insist that *two years* of college education will be needed for "minimum workplace literacy."[3] In terms of full degrees, it's estimated that one-third of all jobs will call for a full four-year degree, and some will also require advanced post-graduate degrees.[4]

While the exact number may vary, everyone is in agreement that advanced education will be necessary to get decent work and to build a decent career. "If you don't have much education, all the trends are that your wages will decline," says David Heer, associate director of the University of Southern California's Population Research Laboratory.[5]

Although education requirements are rapidly increasing and new education opportunities, like apprenticeships, are expanding, the number of people actually being adequately educated and trained in the United States is decreasing. *Today, one-third of the entire adult population of the United States is estimated to be functionally illiterate, unable to read or write at an eighth-grade level.*[6] The U.S. Labor Secretary's Commission on Achieving Necessary Skills estimates that 60 percent of Americans between the ages of 21 and 25 lack the basic reading and writing skills that will be needed in the new workplace.[7]

In *Thinking for a Living*, authors Ray Marshall and Marc Tucker write, "Our front-line workers—those non-managerial and non-technical positions, working directly on the plant floor or in direct contact with customers, on whom we will depend to produce the turnaround in productivity on which our future depends—may be the least skilled among those of all the major industrial nations."[8]

In 1991, Chevron created 30 new jobs at one of its refineries and had over 1,000 applicants for these 30 positions (the effect of recessionary times). Even more startling than the number of applicants was that 75 percent flunked the basic education screening test administered by Chevron.[9] Similarly, a recent study of small businesses showed that more than 10 million workers, or 40 percent of the nation's small business workers, had difficulties performing their jobs because of poor reading, writing and mathematical skills.[10]

A look at the high school education picture in the United States clearly, and sadly, shows where the problem starts. Nationwide, the high school drop-out rate is 29 percent.[11] In inner cities and among minority groups it can be as high as 60 percent.[12] In Boston, for example, four out of every 10 students drop out. Of the six that graduate, three are estimated to be functionally illiterate.[13] Nationally, on an average day, 2,200 kids drop out of high school in this country.[14]

A Shortage of Educated People

The demand for more educated people, coupled with the drop in the number of people getting educated (not to mention the low quality of education that many who stay in school do receive), is causing a strange phenomenon. In the midst of all the layoffs and restructuring that business is experiencing, *there is going to be a labor shortage in this country because we won't have enough skilled, educated workers.*

Further, this shortage will be worsened by the so-called "birth dearth." Fewer people have been born since the baby boom of 1946 to 1964. In 1980, 30 million Americans were between the ages of 19 to 24. But by 1995, only 24 million Americans will be in this age group, which means fewer people will be entering the workforce.[15]

Making the Most of the Education Situation

For many people, this labor shortage can be a plus in advancing their careers *if they take advantage of the situation by furthering their education.* Virtually everyone needs to get more education or training, regardless of their age, field or career level. Educated workers do better in their careers than less educated ones, even in hard times. For example, while the wages of every demographic group dropped during the early 1990s recession, college graduates fared the best with an overall average salary drop of only 3.1 percent, as compared to a 4.4 percent drop among all white-collar workers. This advantage is expected to continue. ". . . A lot of well-educated or technically trained newcomers will do well in the 1990s and beyond," says the Economic Policy Institute, "because their relatively rare skills will command high wages and will be in demand."[16]

The education shortage will also benefit groups that traditionally have had problems getting employed. It is predicted that many people, such as older workers, women re-entering the workforce, minorities, immigrants, retired workers and the disabled, which (historically and unjustly) have been regarded as less desirable in the workforce, will suddenly be in demand if they have or can obtain the necessary education.

Taking a Fresh Look at Learning

Taking advantage and becoming part of the educated workforce in demand means letting go of old assumptions about who should get advanced education and when they should get it. Actually, the classic stereotypes of who is going to school and when, are already disappearing. According to the U.S. Department of Education, the proportion of college students over age 25 was 43 percent in 1989, as compared with 28 percent in 1970. Forty-five to 55-year-olds are predicted to be the fastest growing age segment returning to college.[17] At the community college level, the average age of students enrolled in evening programs is 38, not 18 or 19.[18]

Education Alternatives

The level and kind of education you choose usually depends upon your choice of occupation, where you are in your career or what's happening in certain industries. While decisions vary based on individual needs and timing, some information about the career world in general can be useful in helping you get your bearings.

How much education you feel you need is one consideration. For certain jobs, a four-year degree is the best preparation. Two-year associate degrees from community colleges and certificate-producing vocational and trade schools can provide good training for many professions, such as computer programming, travel services, cosmetology and hotel management.

In a number of fields, an apprenticeship program is a good educational investment. Although underplayed in the United

States, "earn-while-you-learn" apprenticeships have been a major form of education in many European countries, like Germany and Denmark. The United States is beginning to provide more apprenticeship opportunities. While in the past, about 70 percent of the registered 300,000 apprentices in the United States were in the construction industry, today apprenticeship programs are rapidly being created for professions like computer programming, cooking, health care, child care, bank tellers and customer service.[19]

At some point, pursuing a master's degree may be beneficial in a number of occupations, including executive or financial business positions, professional occupations, such as librarians or social workers, and technical specialists, like engineers and architects.[20] Based on upcoming predicted shortages in fields like engineering and natural science, continuing on and obtaining a doctorate can almost be an insurance policy for career success in some fields. Of course, many professions, by their nature, require doctorate-level education, such as law and medicine.[21]

Some fields of study may be more in demand than others. Individuals educated in science and engineering will be particularly critical to the success of the American economy. "American competitiveness," states *Fortune* magazine, "depends on engineers; . . . [the] battle for global market share [is being] fought in corporate R&D labs, and engineers are front-line troops."[22] College graduates with degrees in chemical and electrical engineering are averaging 50 to 75 percent more in earnings than those with degrees in humanities. In 1993, college graduates in petroleum, chemical and mechanical engineering, computer science, physics and nursing received the highest starting-salary offers.[23]

If you are not technically inclined, there is still good news. Many educators and business people strongly believe in the value of a liberal arts, humanities-oriented education. While the immediate financial rewards are not as great (average starting salary for humanities majors in 1992 was around

$21,900 to $22,500[24] as compared to $38,568 for engineering majors[25]), many feel that the skills learned are critical in pursuing a successful career. Stanley Gault, head of Rubbermaid, Inc., says, "A good liberal arts education produces generalists who can think critically and creatively, exercise judgment, sort through complexities, tolerate ambiguity, communicate effectively and adapt to change."[26] Ann Howard and Douglas Bray, industrial psychologists who consult to the Bell System, have found that, ". . . managers who major in the humanities and the social sciences are the strongest in performance, and a greater proportion are apt to be promoted to higher levels within the organization."[27]

Humanities majors, once confined to professions like teaching or journalism, can now expand their career options. Many of the major pharmaceutical companies actively recruit humanities majors for sales positions, even though they do not have a scientific background. These companies value good communication skills and, once a person is hired, fill in scientific blanks through their extensive training programs. Liberal arts graduates are also finding positions in advertising, public relations, banking and computer software development, in addition to traditional areas, like publishing.

Whatever field you pursue, it is a good idea to acquire some technical skills. Princeton economist Alan Krueger claims that anyone who uses a computer generally will earn 15 percent more than equally skilled co-workers who are not computer literate.[28] A graduate in accounting who knows computing well enough to tie two different computerized accounting systems together, for example, is more valuable than one with minimal computer experience.

Another strategy is to combine areas of study. Some colleges are setting up programs to allow students to gain more than one area of expertise. At the University of California at Irvine, social science majors can earn a concurrent minor in business administration.[29] *Time* magazine notes that some American colleges are placing "more emphasis on . . . science and technology, particularly in courses aimed not at those who intend to major in chemistry or engineering, but at liberal arts majors who need at least some scientific literacy."[30] Similarly, the study of more than one foreign language is being encouraged, especially in previously understressed, but now "need-to-know" languages like Chinese, Japanese and Russian.[31]

About MBAs

There has been a lot of hoopla about earning an MBA (master of business administration) degree. In the 1980s, an MBA degree became one of the most coveted degrees in the history of education, with businesses wanting to hire professionally trained managers, marketers and finance people. The number of schools offering an MBA degree and the number of students earning them exploded. As many already in the workforce rushed to get the degree, schools developed specially tailored MBA executive programs, jumping the number of "weekend warriors" to 9,500 in 1992, an increase of 27 percent from 1988.[32] In 1992, 75,000 MBA degrees were granted, up from 5,700 in 1962. They accounted for 25 percent of all master's degrees awarded in the United States.[33]

There is considerable debate about the current value of an MBA degree. Many feel that the market is saturated; overall demand for middle managers is down and will probably remain so. As a result, corporate recruiting is down virtually at all business schools. Ten years ago, the average MBA graduate had 3.8 job offers, now that figure is closer to one. At some schools, one out of five MBA candidates does not receive a job offer by graduation.[34]

In addition to longer job searches, MBA holders are finding salaries may be lower than they once were. Boston University graduates in 1990 are said to have received offers averaging $45,000 to $50,000, but in 1992, $35,000 was the norm.[35] At other schools, the entry-level salary for MBAs with non-technical undergraduate degrees was $32,672, down 10 percent from 1989.[36]

In light of the diminishing demand and appreciation for the MBA degree, before signing up for courses, carefully weigh the degree's potential benefits against the considerable effort and cost required to obtain one. Going for the degree may be a good idea early in your career if research into your field shows it is what employers are looking for, and it can help you compete for the better entry-level jobs. An MBA can also be helpful if you're changing careers. If you're switching from medicine to pharmaceuticals marketing, for example, an MBA can show serious intent on your part and may prove to be a value-added benefit.

If you do decide to pursue the degree, choose a reputable school. Where you get your MBA may weigh more heavily with a potential employer than whether or not you have one. Some companies feel many of the newer schools that "sprung up" in response to demand for the degree offer inferior education, serving as "degree mills" that churn out uneducated students with high expectations, but few management skills.

Even programs at the best business schools are being scrutinized as companies see these schools turning out narrowly focused specialists, while the drastically changed workplace is demanding multifaceted generalists, team players rather than middle-management bosses.

Business schools are responding to the doubts of the corporate world by changing their philosophies and curriculum. Even top-rated Harvard Business School is conducting an extensive formal evaluation of its curriculum. Some schools, like Indiana University, have gotten rid of the traditional core of finance, marketing, accounting and statistics classes and replaced them with cross-disciplinary classes such as "Creativity and Critical Thinking." At Pennsylvania's highly-regarded Wharton School, marketing and finance classes are taught concurrently using the same case studies. Other schools are incorporating field experience into their programs. At the University of Michigan's School of Business Administration, first-year students participate in a field-study program, working on-site in quarter-long business "residencies," where they deal with problems in accessing information systems and manufacturing. Participating companies include General Motors, Xerox, Intel, Philips and Chrysler.[37] MBA students at the University of Tennessee's College of Business Administration spend their first year running "Volunteer Vegetables," a hypothetical company, instead of taking traditional first-year courses.[38]

Also being questioned is the benefit of experience versus theoretical learning, as companies find that MBA graduates whose education is not tempered with real-world experience don't perform that well on the job. For this reason, if you are towards the middle or end of your career, an MBA may not have as much impact on your advancement as your experience might. "[Employers] want field experience," says executive search firm general manager Ron Nery. "If you're in your late twenties, an MBA might help you, but people look at what you've done in the last eight years."[39]

A certificate program at a reputable university can often be a good alternate to pursuing an MBA. Many schools offer programs in a number of fields such as marketing, city planning or public relations. Certificate programs that target your field require less time and money, bring you up-to-date and, depending upon your area of expertise, the certificate earned may produce similar results as an MBA in helping advance your career.

The Boost of Short-Term Programs

Short-term educational programs, including individual classes, seminars and workshops, shouldn't be discounted as valuable education and training. Although education is gained in smaller increments than in full-degree programs, when these increments of education and training are added up, they can have an equal or even greater impact on career success than formal degree programs.

People are taking courses in areas as diverse as computers, accounting, marketing, finance, business writing and exotic foreign languages, such as Arabic and Korean. Even a single class or workshop can make a difference in your career. A community college class in automated spreadsheet programs, for example, can help a secretary move into a financial analyst position. Seminars in sales techniques or time management workshops can advance the sales career, as well as renew the enthusiasm and creativity, of a long-time salesperson.

Employer-Provided Training

The value of employer-provided training programs is often dismissed by employees. They are written off as insignificant, with workers saying, "but my company provided it, so it wasn't like really going to school." This is definitely a misconception. It is estimated that employer-provided training will make up the biggest segment of worker education in the 1990s. As jobs grow more complex, people must learn new technical and conceptual skills; and as jobs change, periodic additional training is necessary to stay current. While any kind of job training will make you more salable to an organization, if the training provided is *occupation-specific* rather than *company-specific*, the long-term career benefits are greater.

Providing job training is a new role for many American companies. Only one out of every 14 American workers receives formal job training that involves little more than just "following Joe around."[40] As of early 1993, a mere 15,000 of the total workforce benefited from 90 percent of the $30 billion spent annually on training.[41] By contrast, employer-provided training is standard practice in many countries. Germany and Denmark have extensive apprenticeship programs. Japanese businesses are expected to provide in-depth employee training. Toyota, for example, developed a program for new hires just out of school. Before they even work on the assembly line, these new employees are put through a two-year, full-time course in digital electronics and mechatronics. This training results in Toyota's assembly-line workers having the same qualifications as junior engineers in the United

States.[42] Japanese business culture is, of course, much different from that in the U.S. Although the recent recession in Japan is causing the country's first layoffs, employment with a company is generally regarded as a lifetime bond, making it cost-effective for companies like Toyota to invest large sums in training.

Even though work tenure is different in the United States, training programs are essential to keep American employees as productive as those of our global competitors. Jack Welch, CEO of General Electric, says, "Within GE, we've got to upgrade workers' skills through intense and continuous training. Companies can't promise lifetime employment, but by constant training and education we may be able to guarantee lifetime employability. We've got to invest totally in our people."[43]

Training does pay off. Studies conducted by the American Society of Training and Development show that job training to improve an employee's technical skills typically triples a person's productivity.[44] Other studies show that formally trained workers earn 20 to 30 percent more than those who aren't trained, and that they have fewer periods of unemployment.[45]

Starbuck Coffee Co. has had a compounded annual growth rate of 80 percent for three years running. According to Howard Schultz, CEO and president, employee training is the strategy that has made the difference. "Our only sustainable competitive advance is the quality of our workforce," Schultz claims. "We're building a national retail company by creating pride in—and a stake in—the outcome of our labor." Each Starbuck employee averages 25 hours of classroom training time. And training is provided to all employees, even though over half of the retail sales force is comprised of part-time workers.[46]

Productivity rose 200 percent over a four-year period at a Motorola plant manufacturing personal pagers, while the manufacturing staff only increased by 22 percent. Hector Ruiz, general manager, says, "The factory doesn't look much different. The improvement came about through training. Our return on training is on the order of 30-to-1."[47] Rather than laying off workers, Motorola has cut costs $3.3 billion since 1987 by training workers companywide in how to simplify processes and reduce waste. Profits are up 47 percent and sales per employee have doubled in the last five years.[48]

The quality of some corporate training programs rivals that of the best business schools. Many team up with outside educators and consultants. Weyerhaeuser, the Washington-based wood and paper company, saw its profits in wood products slipping, and determined that it had become too large and bureaucratic—customers were finding it easier to buy from smaller competitors. Horace Park, Weyerhaeuser's head of executive education, called in James Bolt, former head of human-resources planning at Xerox and current chairman of Executive Development Associates. Together, they formed the Leadership Institute for Managers, a training entity within the company. The Institute focused on teaching a customer-oriented style of management. After training 1,240 of its managers, division profits were in the black, even with the $11 million cost of the program. And customers commented on finding the company easier to do business with.[49]

Optimizing Your Future

However acquired, all educational experiences are vitally important. They help you keep your skills updated and enhance your value in the workplace. In addition to being personally fulfilling, ongoing education and training allow you to optimize your job performance, move into new areas and make proactive career choices.

PART THREE:
PAVING NEW GROUND

8. E*XPLORING NEW OPTIONS*

I f having a traditional job in the large corporate world is not to your liking, you may want to look into working for a small organization or becoming a telecommuter in a large one. Part-time or temporary employment may also be choices to consider if you don't need to work full time.

The Small-Business Option

Small businesses, defined by the Small Business Administration (SBA) as manufacturing or service companies with 500 or less employees, are an important part of our economy. They have been the major source—80 percent—of all new jobs created since the early 1980s.[1] Between 1988 and 1990, businesses employing 500 or less added a net 3.2 million jobs to the economy, while big businesses had a net loss of 500,000 jobs.[2] Today there are roughly 20.5 million small businesses, up from 12 million in 1977.[3]

Small companies have much to offer. Often, they have been started by experienced executives with *lots* of savvy, many of whom were thrust out of the corporate world by restructurings. Because these companies are new and small, they are usually in touch with their marketplace so their products and services can be right on the mark. Their size also allows them to react quickly to changes in the marketplace.

Small companies, for example, can often create and introduce new products faster than big businesses. This may be because senior management is in more direct communication with front-line salespeople, or simply that having fewer (and, therefore, more productive) employees involved in the development of a new product tends to speed up the process.

In a small company, there's usually a strong sense of teamwork and camaraderie. It's tough to beat the enthusiastic (and demanding) atmosphere generated by a group of people who are tightly bonded together and committed to "making it happen." Studies by *Inc.* magazine show that people in companies with 50 to 100 employees were happier than those in larger firms.[4] One reason may be that with fewer layers of management, it can be easier to gain diverse experience quickly and carve out a "fast track." Since they can't offer the prestige of working for a large, established firm, small companies may compensate by offering hard cash or innovative bonus programs that would be prohibited in a large, bureaucratic compensation structure. You can manage your career more directly in a small firm, says career expert Marilyn Moats Kennedy. Since ". . . there is no bureaucracy, [and] top management knows everyone, [you] can make a pitch for promotion right to the CEO or owner."[5]

The disadvantages of opting to work for a small company bear mentioning as well. They can topple over faster than big companies because they don't have established financial resources to carry them through hard times. Overall, they pay 10 to 13 percent less for comparable work with larger employers.[6] Small companies are less likely to offer important benefits like health insurance, and the quality of the benefits they do provide may not be as good as those offered by the bigger firms. Because there are fewer people, most employees wear several hats and the pressure to perform can sometimes be intense. Thus, there is a higher risk of burning out just from the sheer amount of work and number of hours people put in.

In a small company you have to be your own advocate. The same lack of bureaucracy that makes it a great place to work can also mean there is no formal salary or performance review system. Few small companies can afford or need human resources staff. This means that you have to campaign hard to have your work recognized and to get ahead. Besides not having a personnel staff to look out for you, you may also find your boss too busy to notice your accomplishments if you don't point them out.

If a company is family-owned, be cautious. It may be a great business and they may be a great group of people, but "blood is thicker than water," and you have the inherent disadvantage of always being an outsider.

It is highly likely you will be working for a small company at some point in your career. Today, small businesses account for the employment of 57 percent of America's workers, and this percentage is expected to grow. William J. Morin, president of Drake Beam Morin outplacement services, says that the country's smallest firms—those with five to 25 workers—may, in fact, be the likeliest places to find jobs.[7]

The Telecommuting Option

Telecommuting can be a nice alternative to the corporate "rat race." While most people tend to think of a telecommuter as someone working at home with a computer, there is really no clear definition.

One way to define "telecommuter" is to include everyone who does some part of his or her professional work at home. This segment makes up approximately 39 million Americans,[8] but their circumstances vary greatly:

- "Homeworkers" make up the largest segment of the 39 million. These 8.6 million people bring work home from the office and do it after normal business hours.[9]

- Thirty-one percent, or 12.1 million of all self-employed people work from home-based, rather than outside, office-based businesses.

- Another 11.7 million people hold more than one job and work at home part of the time.[10]

- The smallest segment of homeworkers, 6.6 million, actually fit the general conception of true tele-commuters: employees who work at home, but are linked to companies by telephone, fax, modem and personal computer.[11] And of this group, most do only part of their work at home, perhaps one or two days a week. The actual number who work *full time* at home is only about 1.5 million.[12]

As with all career choices, teleccmmuting, part or full time, has its pluses and minuses. Employees and employers like it because people often get more done when they work at home uninterrupted. Some studies show home-based data entry workers complete their tasks 10 times faster than they do in the office.[13] In a pilot test, Chicago Illinois Bell telephone company found the productivity of at-home customer service representatives 40 percent higher than its in-office staff.[14]

As with at-home work in general, telecommuting allows you to have more control over your work pattern, can eliminate a long commute and can afford high-quality, reduced-stress work time without the interruptions that occur in a typical work environment. On the other hand, if it is to succeed, you have to be motivated, plan well and stick to your plans. Also, it's easy to feel isolated, say home workers, or feel like you never get away from work, since ". . . [your] papers and other materials tend to infiltrate the whole house."[15]

If you decide telecommuting is for you, be careful. "Out-of-sight-out-of mind" can mean you don't get chosen for certain projects, miss out on key assignments, or worst of all, aren't included in the promotional process. A vice president for a New York City-based financial firm who works from her home in the Midwest says, "By the same token that you're less victimized by office politics and office bores, you are less informed about what is going on. You have to have strong relationships with colleagues and others in order to keep up, and you have to work harder and take more initiative to generate your assignments, which won't *just fall your way because you happen to be there.*"[16] Stay in touch with people in your office, if it's appropriate, whether by meeting for lunch or talking on the phone. Don't "disappear." You still want to be considered part of the team, and you want to be kept in the loop with what's going on.

Many managers don't want to work at home because they fear their low visibility will hurt their career and that their staff won't get the work done. Managers also worry about their employees who work at home. They can be uncomfortable not knowing when the employee is actually working and become concerned that work won't get done right or be done at all. They worry telecommuters will lose touch with supervisors and lose sight of corporate goals. Management concerns such as these strongly affect telecommuting programs. The number-one challenge of telecommuting is to convince managers to buy off on the concept, says Wendell Joice, a personnel psychologist for the U.S. Office for Personnel Management.[17]

To allay management concerns and maintain control over your career, it's important to stay in touch. Be sure you keep your boss, co-workers or anyone else who needs to know informed of your goals, objectives and progress. Clarify how often you should check in on a day-to-day basis, whether it be in person, by phone or some other means of communication. In some situations, it may be appropriate to find out if your employer will be visiting your at-home work site. If so, determine if these will be scheduled visits, or if you might have "surprise walk-ins."

Be realistic. Unless you actually are located some distance from work (like in another city or state), most companies will want you to be at their work location part of the time. If you are the one pushing for telecommuting, be willing to negotiate and expect to have to go into the office some of the time. It helps if you already have a good track record of performance you can use to assure them of your productivity. And do your homework. Think through the advantages and benefits your employer will gain by your working at home. Be prepared to answer questions and objections.

Communication between employer and employee is a key issue in making telecommuting work. Get everything worked out as much as possible before you start. When negotiating the terms of your telecommuting with your employer, be sure all the logistics are well defined. Find out if your compensation, benefits and career advancement will be affected. Work with your employer to establish clear, mutually agreed-upon criteria for judging your work and performance. And after you've put the deal together, get something in writing.

If you are a union member, you will have to get permission from your union. This can be quite difficult. Worried that their members will be given too much work, unequal pay or will be passed over for advancement, unions have traditionally not been in favor of telecommuting. This is beginning to change. Kathleen Christensen, a professor at City University of New York and specialist in work-at-home arrangements, reports that some unions are participating in pilot telecommuting programs, and unions in general are becoming more receptive to the idea.[18]

Explain to your family and friends what you are doing. You don't want them to think that you are easy to interrupt or available to run errands just because you are at home. Sometimes, the people in your life can become jealous of your situation. If you are getting comments like, "So what do you do on your day off?" or "How's your vacation going?" or "Your time is your own, so why not be the one to coordinate the homeowners' association meeting?"—it may be time to clear up some critical misunderstandings.

When you set up your work office, be sure it's adequate. Make certain you have all the work materials, data and office supplies you need. You can miss a critical deadline if you suddenly find you didn't bring home an essential report, or your printer just ran out of toner.

Be prepared to make changes and modifications as situations arise. Remember that in order for telecommuting to work, both the employee and employer have to voluntarily agree to it and actively participate in the process.

The Working-Part-Time and Temping Options

Part-time work: For those who don't need a full-time income, part-time work can be a good choice and is often preferred by older workers, parents with small children and students. In 1990, the U.S. Bureau of Labor reported that 15.2 million workers chose to work part time, up from 14.2 million in 1980.[19] Many firms, such as department stores, banks, grocery stores, health care providers and telemarketing companies routinely hire part-time workers as a large part of their total staff.

Some companies are offering employees the option of part-time work in order to be able to hire and keep good people who want flexible schedules, such as women and older workers. "College-educated women and women with technical specialties are going to be in the best position ever," says business consultant Joan Lloyd. "There aren't going to be enough of them, so employers are going to fight to hire them, and in order to keep them they're going to bend over backward."[20] At Aetna Life & Casualty, for example, employees can work as few as 15 hours a week and still keep full benefit packages. The company, in fact, uses this policy as a recruiting tool. "This helps us keep good workers," says Michelle Carpenter, manager of work and family strategies. "Since finding and replacing employees is so expensive, we're contributing to the company's bottom line."[21]

Other firms offer part-time employment to reduce costs. Some industries, like banking and shipping, are finding they save money with part-time staff by paying less in wages and providing reduced (or no) benefits.[22] Also, part-time workers allow companies to staff up for peak work times without having a lot of people on the payroll during slower periods. Since its purchase of Security Pacific National Bank, Bank of America reports that fewer than 10 percent of its tellers now work full time. "We're open more than 50 hours a week in most of our branches," says Richard Beebe, spokesperson for the bank. "We're staffing so that we have the flexibility to bring staff in during peak hours."[23]

If you choose to work part time, the opportunities are great. If you want to work full time, but can only find part-time opportunities, take them and continue to look for full-time employment. Sometimes a part-time job can be a good way to get your foot in the door, because it can turn into a full-time position. Part-time work as a stopgap measure allows you the time to pursue another position, even if it means your overall schedule will be pretty full. If need be, working two part-time jobs may keep you afloat until you find a full-time opportunity.

Temporary Work: Traditionally, temporary workers— "temps" as they are generally called—are thought of as clerical workers, or fill-in secretaries and receptionists who come in when the "regular" person is out sick, on vacation or has left unexpectedly. **The scope of temping has broadened in the new workplace.** There are even interim management firms specializing in placing managers in temporary positions. Today, temping can include work on a professional or executive level by attorneys, sales managers, marketing executives and scientists. It can also mean working on a temporary assignment or being hired part time through an outside contractor to do computer programming, accounting or engineering. In 1993, temporary workers (including traditional "temps," independent contractors, part-timers, and freelancers) accounted for 25 percent of the workforce, up from 12 percent in 1983.[24] According to the National Association of Temporary Services, the temp industry itself was the third-fastest growing industry in the United States in 1991 with about 4,000 temporary employment agencies placing over one million workers daily.[25] In 1993, the number of temp agencies expanded significantly to as many as 7,000,[26] making a daily placement of 1.5 million workers.[27]

Company restructuring is behind much of the boom in temporary employment. Many downsized companies are finding they still need some of the expertise they let go. One solution is to bring in temporary workers for specific projects or time periods. "Companies are being forced to get creative," says Mark Alch, senior vice president with outplacement firm Drake Beam Morin, Inc. "They had to cut costs so they reduced their workforces, but they found the work didn't always go away. The reality is many companies now have to bring back the expertise."[28] Temping is one way to do this.

Temping has some unique advantages. It can be a good way to gain valuable experience. In Los Angeles, many film school graduates work for Our Gang, a temporary employment agency specializing in the entertainment industry. "They're hoping it will lead to something bigger, and a lot of times it does," says Our Gang job counselor Kim Marsh. "There are people we've placed in clerical jobs that have ended up doing quite well in the business."[29]

Some people find that temping can be a way to explore new career directions. Audrey Freedman, president of the New York consulting firm Manpower Plus, says with so many businesses looking for temporary or contingent employees, workers have far more opportunity to try on different hats and find the right match for their skills and interests. "People have hobbies and skills they don't yet realize can be channeled into productive work," Freedman says.[30]

Temping also shares the merits of part-time work. For some, like older workers, parents and students, it's a good alternative to working full time. For others, it can be a stopgap measure until a full time position can be found.

Look into temping as an alternative, regardless of your field. Temporary agencies exist for almost every profession: Lawsmiths in San Francisco places attorneys; Bank Temps in Denver fills loan officer slots; On Assignment Inc., based in California, has 27 offices nationwide and supplies scientists; and IMCOR is a Connecticut-based firm that specializes in senior executives who are expert at turnaround situations.[31]

Using New Options to Build Your Career

If you are planning a career move, include nontraditional options in your career strategies. Working for a small company, telecommuting, taking a part-time job or temping have helped some former corporate workers build a new career in a nontraditional setting or role. While these alternative measures are often used as a way to keep bread on the table until a more traditional position can be found, some people use them as a path to being hired by a large employer. In all of these cases, it's important to be flexible and open to new possibilities. And, much like the Star Trek heroes, you must be willing "to go where no person has gone before."

9. ⬛⬛⬛   GOING ON YOUR OWN

I' ve always had this great idea for starting a business." "I want to work for myself and be my own boss." "I'm sick of working for someone else." Most everyone has thoughts of being on their own: from senior-level executives who want to run their own show, to technicians who prefer to decide where and how they provide their expertise, to professionals or blue-collar workers with a strong outside interest they want to turn into a business. And in today's workplace, "being on your own" is becoming a popular option.

The Many Paths to Entrepreneurship

Most men and women who make the entrepreneurial choice are influenced by changes happening in the workplace. A drastically reduced number of management positions, the disappearance of "fast tracks" and promotional opportunities, and the growing trend of companies to buy outside services from individuals and small businesses are often influencing factors.

Often, laid-off managers and professionals decide they don't want to put themselves "at risk" in another corporate position where their destiny is totally out of their hands. Outplacement firm Challenger, Gray & Christmas reports that one out of every five laid-off managers they counsel starts his or her own business. "More than 70 percent are over 40," says president James Challenger. "Becoming their own boss is preferable to going back on another payroll. They fear the emotional trauma of being discharged again."[1]

Some people, when faced with unemployment, find it is an opportune time to do something they've always wanted to do. Mary Anne Jackson, former director of business-and-operations planning for Swift/Eckrich, a division of Beatrice Foods, started a business, called My Own Meals. When she lost her job, her husband encouraged her to go on her own, telling her she had nothing to lose. Jackson says, "I knew if I passed it by, I would probably have kicked myself."[2]

Those not finding the kind of advancement opportunities they had expected in their current job are also starting their own shops. This is particularly true of baby boomers, whose career movement was halted by too many people competing for too few management positions. "Baby boomers grew up with expectations that just can't be fulfilled," says Judy Bardwick, Ph.D., author of *The Plateauing Trap*.[3] In 1975, a typical middle-management position had 10 potential candidates; that number is expected to rise to 30 by 1995[4] and to 50 in the year 2000.[5]

What Kind of Business to Start

Starting your own venture may mean simply sharing your expertise. While in the past, the term "consultant" often implied "out-of-work," today consulting has earned new respect and promise in the workplace and is growing as companies find it more cost-effective to *contract out* than *hire in*. In 1991, American businesses spent an estimated $13.5 billion on consulting services.[6] Currently, almost 1.3 million people classify themselves as consultants,[7] selling every service imaginable from agricultural services to zoo management.[8] These consultants market their expertise to their industries. Often, in the case of laid-off workers, they market them back to the employer that laid them off. Some studies estimate that as many as one-third of those laid off turn around and market their services back to their former employer. "As corporations disaggregate, huge markets are opening up for precisely the people who are being displaced," says Charles Handy, author and professor at the London Business School.[9]

It is not uncommon today to find people utilizing their expertise to start businesses similar to those of their former employers, often specializing in more closely defined market niches. In certain industries, such as biotechnology, there are even companies that provide funds to former employees to start their own businesses supplying adjunct products and services. In these "strategic alliances," the new business opens with an assured first customer, and the large company has a new way to get the product or service more cost-effectively.

Those who prefer not to "invent" a new business can always tap into a business concept developed by others and buy a franchise. Franchising is a $246 billion industry and accounts for roughly 25 percent of new businesses started every year.[10] Franchises are authorized spin-offs of someone's business ideas and business strategies.[11] When they are successful, franchises can offer less of a risk than starting from scratch because you get a blueprint for what to do.[12] Most of us know about franchises like Pizza Hut or Burger King. But there are over 2,000 other franchised companies in more than 60 industries, such as home remodeling, carpet cleaning, painting, dry cleaning, temporary employment agencies and auto service centers, and some unusual ones, like Air Boingo (steel bungee-jumping towers) and Strictly Shooting (gun shops).[13]

A successful franchise can be a great business for the right person. According to the U.S. Small Business Administration, franchises have a 5-percent first-year failure rate as compared to 30 percent for small businesses in general.[14] And, suggests John James, director of entrepreneurial services at Arthur Young, ". . . a corporate team player may be better for franchising than an entrepreneurial maverick who doesn't like rules and procedures imposed by franchisers."[15]

Should you opt to buy a franchise, look into it carefully.

Even with reputable franchisers, there can be disputes between franchiser and franchisee over sufficient delivery of promised start-up and ongoing support. Be sure you understand all the terms, such as exactly how much support will be given and how many restrictions or how much freedom you will have.

What Comes With the Bargain

Before you decide to start your own business, you should be aware of the risks involved. According to the U.S. Small Business Administration, *63 percent of all small businesses fail in the first six years.*[16]

Even businesses that technically don't fail may have a tough time of it. While most of us envision growing profits and increasing success, the reality is that many new business start-ups that don't fail outright often stagnate. Sixty percent of all U.S. businesses bring in *gross revenues of $25,000 or less a year.* And five to six years later, they are typically still at that same revenue level.[17]

Thinking It Through

The decision to start your own business needs to be well-thought-out. Important factors include:

- Assessing your skills, experience, personality, temperament and work style, as well as your financial and personal situations.

- Exploring and understanding the different self-employment options, such as consulting versus starting a small, labor-intensive manufacturing facility requiring investment capital.

- Understanding what's happening in the workplace.

- Taking a thorough look into what it will be like to be on your own.

Dealing With Your Identity

Making the transition from an organization person to an entrepreneur entails enormous change. People identify with their work world and their place in it. A client of mine left his position as vice president of marketing with a large financial services firm to start his own consulting business. He said that for months after he left, when people asked him what he did, he would begin by saying, "Well, I used to be a corporate vice president." It was hard for him to break his identification with the corporate world.

If you've been laid off, the transition can be particularly hard as you nurse a bruised ego, deal with your emotions and come to terms with the loss of your corporate status. And the absence of taken-for-granted job niceties, like secretaries, corporate perks and travel, can be traumatic as you learn to adjust.

In order to get on with the process, you have to let go. You need to forget that you were a strategic planner for a large company or a computer programmer with a small but prestigious one. And while you will be the top executive of your new firm, you need to accept that very likely you will also be the bookkeeper and janitor.

Are You the Entrepreneurial Type?

Numerous studies have been conducted to determine who makes a successful entrepreneur. In all of these, many of the same questions are posed regarding the basics of successful entrepreneurship:

What Is Your Risk Tolerance?

First off, are you a risk-taker? Are you comfortable making fast decisions? How do you react when things change unexpectedly? What would be your response if you found you'd made some very wrong decisions? How well can you mentally recoup from financial or other losses? If you get dry-mouthed just reading these questions, owning your own business may not be a great idea. "Some people are not risk-takers," says Don DeVore, head of Corporate Executive Outplacement Group in Pasadena, California. "Starting a business not only takes liquidity, but you also have to be willing to tie up your house, your car, your spouse, your cat and dog."[18]

Do You Like to Be Alone?

Starting your own business almost always means working by yourself a great deal of the time, especially in the beginning. Will this work for you? Think about your past job and about your life in general. Do you usually work and spend leisure time with other people? If you do, is this what you prefer, or do you wish you had more time on your own? Do you enjoy time spent alone?

If you prefer to be with people or don't work well when you're alone, this can be a problem. Isolation is one of the three top difficulties cited by people who own their own business. One way to compensate is to plan time with people. Set up lunch or after-work dates with business contacts or friends. Join a professional organization. In some areas, there are even support groups for self-employed individuals.

Another strategy is to consider whether you want to take on a partner. Some form of partnering or joining with others can be a good solution, but approach it carefully. Partnerships and business ownerships are just like marriages and have all of the same benefits and risks.

How Motivated Are You?

To start and run your own business, you need a great deal of motivation. You must be able to conceptualize, bring ideas into reality and perform the day-to-day "business of running a business" on your own. This requires getting going in the morning, day after day, and getting things done under your own steam. This is tough. Entrepreneurs *average* 60- to 69-hour workweeks, with many working well above that.[19] Again, look at past jobs and other areas of your life to evaluate how self-motivated you are.

Is There a Need for Your Product or Service?

Test the waters to determine if you have a market. Do some research into supply and demand. The greatest product or service in the world won't be a success if no one wants to buy it.

One rule of thumb is to go into a business that you know something about. Although people do make successful leaps into the unknown, it's a good idea to have your business based on *something* you already know, some aspect of your experience, skills and training. This can be a physical product, like computers; a service, like accounting; an industry, like food services; or a skill, like marketing, that you are applying to another industry. But somewhere in there should be something that you already know. In a study conducted by American Express Small Business Services and the National Federation of Independent Businesses, the business survival rate was 80 percent for owners who had previous experience with their product or service as opposed to 72 percent for those who started up in new fields.[20] The Center for the Study of Entrepreneurship at Marquette University found that the majority of start-up companies that experienced rapid growth were headed by CEOs who had more than 10 years of experience in the industry in which they had started their business.[21]

Do You Have the Skills to Run a Business?

Running any kind of business encompasses many areas of responsibility and requires certain skills. What do you know about marketing? Distribution? Accounting? Leasing a building? Handling a payroll? Most of us have some areas of expertise, and other areas are total blanks. Don't panic when you discover gaps in your knowledge and experience. Instead, *fill in the blanks.* Take classes offered through university extension programs or community colleges. Look into the often-excellent free counseling provided by organizations like SCORE (Small Business Core of Retired Executives Association) or AWED (American Woman's Economic Development Corporation). Check into services through the U.S. Small Business Administration (SBA) which sponsors, for example, local Small Business Development Centers[22] and co-sponsors Small Business Institutes on some university campuses.[23]

Do You Have the Financial Resources?

Financing your business requires careful planning, research and logistics. It's a critical, complex process. As you do it, there are a few things to keep in mind. Almost everyone underestimates the amount of capital needed to run a business. *Undercapitalization* is one of the main reasons for small business failures. Remember that you will not have company-provided health insurance, pensions or other benefits. You must figure in the cost of these before you start.

Do Those Closest to You Understand What You Are Getting Into?

Starting a business can put tremendous strain on your personal relationships. The sheer amount of time you put in can cause friction and leave others feeling neglected. The financial commitment and uncertainty may affect everyone involved, causing tension and flare-ups. Even positives, like your enthusiasm, can irritate those close to you who may be jealous of the attention you're putting into your new endeavor. They may feel they don't have your attention or fear you are not progressing quickly enough. If you and a spouse or live-together friend are both involved in the new business, you will have to develop the ability to work together *and* live together, a real art.

While you can't anticipate everything that will happen, try to be sure that everyone close to you understands all the different commitments being made, and keep them current on what's happening. Work hard at maintaining open lines of communication.

How Confident Are You?

Planning is crucial, but confidence is a key success factor in starting your own business. While there will be moments of doubt, you have to have an overriding confidence that you will succeed, and a firm, positive belief in your product or service and your ability to market it. You must demonstrate your confidence to your customers or clients. You are their supplier. If you have chosen a consulting role, the need for confidence is even more critical because you are selling your expertise and your clients should regard you as an authority.

Working at Home Vs. Opening an Outside Office

Unless you have a business that involves manufacturing a complex product or employing 20 telemarketers in one location, you may be considering whether or not to work out of your home. Starting your new business from home can often be a smart move. It holds down your initial investment costs, helps keep your overhead low and can provide tax advantages, according to Kathleen Christensen, director of the National Project on Home-Based Work at New York City University's graduate school.[24]

By the year 2000, one-third of the workforce will be made up of people owning home-based businesses.[25] The home-business market is big enough that companies like AT&T, Sharp Electronics and Canon USA, Inc. are actively pursuing it.[26] No surprise. Technology has spurred its growth. The incredible enhancements made in communications have removed the need for people to work geographically close to one another. Armed with a personal computer, high-quality printer, fax, answering machine or voice mail, you can project almost any image you want to the outside world.

Working out of your home may be a great experience, or it can be a nightmare. Sarah Edwards, co-author of four books about home-based businesses, sums it up, "The biggest advantage is that you're in charge of everything. And the biggest disadvantage is that you're in charge of everything."[27]

You have to deal with feelings of isolation and take on the challenges of staying motivated and disciplined.

Many home-based workers feel they are always at work. After all, it's right there, in the same place where you live. One way to cope is to physically separate your work space from the rest of the house and try to think of it as an office, not part of your home. Some people literally open their "office door" at eight in the morning and close it behind them at five to maintain separateness between work and home. If you don't have a room to allocate, a den or corner of the dining room is preferable to working in the bedroom. "The worst place to set up a home office is in the bedroom," says Edwards. "One woman told us, 'I realized I couldn't even get sick and get away from my business.'"[28]

Another problem can be child care. Many people, particularly women, work at home so they can be with and care for their children. But, it's a tough balance to maintain. While you may be able to supervise your kids, you will most likely need hired help as well. In a survey of 7,000 women who worked at home, two-thirds hired child care. The ones who didn't felt overworked.[29]

Once you work out the kinks, running your business from home can be a great experience and one that has unexpected benefits. In a readership study by *Home Office Computing*, 85 percent of the respondents said they felt more relaxed working from home, 40 percent had a healthier diet, 39 percent took more time off, 38 percent exercised more and 32 percent felt they had improved their marriage or sex life. A whopping 98 percent said they were happier in general, 96 percent would recommend it to others and 88 percent vowed never to return to the corporate world.[30] "You are given control in the most basic sense," says Edwards. "You decide when you get up, when you go to bed, how you pace yourself."[31]

On the Side

Another way to start your own business is to do it "on the side" while you are still employed. The benefit of doing this is that you still have the security of your mainstream job while you go about the adventure of starting up your own show. The main disadvantage, of course, is that you are "moonlighting," working two jobs at once which can certainly take its toll.

If you are still employed, pay close attention to your relationship with your employer. Going into direct competition can cause problems, especially if you signed an employment contract with a non-compete clause when you were hired. "From a legal standpoint, there are definite risks, the biggest being that an employer could sue you for unfair competition," advises attorney Paul Pincus. "All employees," he says, "have an implied 'duty of loyalty,' a responsibility not to engage in any business-related activities that might be harmful to an employer's efforts."[32]

Some companies have formal policies about moonlighting and employee start-ups. These policies can encourage employees or prohibit them. In either case, you need to know what they are so that you can make sensible decisions.

Scary but Rewarding

By whatever route you get there, owning a successful business can be extremely rewarding. True, it is scary, but if you recognize the fear, you can move forward despite it. "Starting your own business is like getting married," says Mary Anne Jackson, founder of My Own Meals. "You never know when you're ready. And you never think you're quite ready."[33]

PART FOUR:

SPECIAL ADVICE FOR SPECIAL GROUPS

10.

COLLEGE GRADUATES

T here's no question that college graduates face a tough job market. The days of graduating from college with one or more job offers already in your pocket are over for most people. Today, when you graduate, you are facing a work world that's been turned on its side, where people and organizations are changing and trying to adjust to change all at the same time. Companies have not only laid off people, they have restructured. They're running with fewer employees while dealing with increased pressure to perform.

This changed workplace substantially impacts college graduates. For most, it is not a world that is rolling out the red carpet and welcoming you with open arms. There are fewer entry-level jobs. Between 1988 and 1992, 750,000 entry-level jobs for college graduates disappeared.[1] Company recruiting through on-campus programs is down 10 to 50 percent, depending on the individual school.[2] In addition, there is more competition than before. Graduates are not only competing with each other for jobs, they are competing with graduates from the year before who are still looking *and* with experienced workers who have been laid off. It is not unusual for an entry-level job advertisement to draw responses from literally *everyone*—graduates new to the workforce and people with 10 years of experience are answering the same ads. At Stowe Engineering Corp., a 90-person firm in Massachusetts, one entry-level engineering ad generated more than 200 respondents, the majority of whom had more than 20 years of experience.[3] "It's kind of hard to get a job in general," laments a 28-year-old Californian with a master's degree in electrical engineering, "because you're going against experienced people who are out of work." [4]

You Can Do It

While all this doom and gloom can be overwhelming and cloud your perspective, it really only means that it is harder to find a job, but not impossible. America's organizations— including corporations, non-profits and government organizations—still need employees. But new and different tactics are required. You have to understand what is needed in the current job climate to be job-competitive. You must:

- Understand what employers are looking for.
- Orient your thinking and adjust your attitudes, if need be.
- Learn how to seriously and persistently look for a job.
- Put more effort into it than you had ever dreamed.
- Have courage, faith and perseverance.

Prepare yourself. Getting this first job may be the hardest thing you've ever done. You must be strong. It's okay to lick your wounds along the way, but this is no place for wimps. Be optimistic. There is much to be gained from your efforts. The skills you develop during your search can immediately be used in your new job. Marketing yourself demands creativity, problem-solving, persistence and strong communication skills. Starting your new job with these tools already honed will help you meet its challenges and speed you on your way to becoming a high-level performer.

Understanding What Makes You Attractive to Employers

With today's abundance of candidates, most companies can be as "choosy" as they want to be. To become one of the

chosen, you must be savvy about what employers are looking for. Employers want people who work hard and *get things
done. They are looking for initiative, the ability to analyze and
make decisions, and want employees who can do more than
one kind of work.* This isn't lip service, it's for real. If a company is going to prosper with fewer employees, each employee
has to count and make a difference. There is no slack left in
today's job market for people who coast along, don't contribute or can't get the job done. "We believe right to our toes
that we've got to engage every mind in this place," says Jack
Welch, CEO of General Electric.[5]

Have the right attitude. Don't grovel and come across
as needy and pathetic with a panicked, "I'll do anything, just
please, please, please hire me" look in your eye. Don't appear
desperate; employers view over-anxious job seekers as less
desirable than confident ones. On the other hand, don't act
like you are higher education's gift to the work world. Sometimes, when you are trying to project confidence, you can
overdo it. If you feel like a quivering bowl of jello inside, don't
overcompensate by coming across as too aggressive and self-
confident. "Arrogance" and "cockiness" was cited as the number-one turnoff by 320 corporate recruiters surveyed by
Northwestern University.[6]

Expect to pay your dues. Although most graduates know
all too well how tough the job market is, there are still a few
souls who expect to cruise right in and not only get hired,
but jump into a high-level position. This probably isn't going
to happen. The old saying of having to pay your dues still
holds true. If you want to be a bank loan officer, you'll probably have to start as a teller. "Something I'm coming to realize is that you have to start at the bottom. I was living under
the illusion that you're going to join the company and get top
salary," says a former graduate, reflecting on how her attitude changed during a tough job search. "I look at my parents and their friends," she continues. "I want to live like them,
but they've been working for 30 years. I never saw them when
they were starving and living in that little apartment."[7]

Have a realistic attitude and make sure it is reflected in your actions and conversation. Don't double-talk and insinuate that the world's not fair or things aren't working out the way you had planned. People out in the world know that and realize plans have to change to fit reality. "[Graduates] say they're willing to pay their dues," observes Gilbert Gatyan of Allegheny Personnel in New York, "but in the same breath, they'll mention 'someone I heard about' who got a fifty-five-thousand-dollar-a-year job as an editorial assistant. Or they'll 'do anything' to get a foot in the door, and then add that their parents didn't spend sixty-thousand dollars on their college education so they could answer phones."[8]

Tracy Salter is someone who had the right attitude. She wanted to work in management for Euro Disney, but was told that the company was not hiring Americans for its European project. She even flew over to London, talked to contacts she had inside the company, applied in person, but was still refused. Finally she changed her strategy. "Maybe I'm aiming too high," she thought. "It seemed as though the key was just getting *any* job. I found out that if you applied for a position that *wasn't* management, it was much easier to get an interview. I was willing to work as a janitor, just to get started." This change of strategy got her an interview and a job. "Once I was inside the door and they realized they could use my language skills, it was clear I wouldn't have to scrub floors." Today, Salter is a park special-activities coordinator for Euro Disney in France.[9]

Learning to Job Hunt

The most important thing you can do is *learn to look for a job and then look for one*, an obvious tactic that often eludes many graduates. There will be many surprises. Remember, the traditional career path of choosing one career and working for one employer is gone. Today, you need to consider an array of options, rather than one or two. Many of these will be choices college graduates traditionally haven't considered, such as working for small or unconventional companies, relocating or taking a public-service job. Or you may opt to continue your education with some kind of graduate training and postpone full-time employment. "With competition for jobs so fierce, students are realizing they have to take a different path to get their dream jobs," notes Victor R. Lindquist, director of placement at Northwestern University.[10]

You need to apply this more-than-one-option strategy to your job-search methods as well, and not limit yourself to the narrow approach used by students in the past. Include less conventional methods, such as contacting companies regardless of whether you know they are hiring as well as the established methods, like signing up for on-campus recruitment programs. Traditional approaches are no longer enough.

Companies surveyed by the College Placement Council in 1993 said they plan to visit 11.3 percent fewer campuses than last year.[11] Students at *all* levels are finding fewer jobs through these programs. Even professional areas like law are being affected. Bill McGeary, director of career services at the University of California Los Angeles Law School, says that three years ago, 90 percent of the school's students had been offered and had accepted positions before their graduation. Now, the number who already have jobs has dropped to 80 percent.[12] On other campuses, "job fairs" are replacing much of the traditional one-on-one interviewing process that provided students with personalized high exposure to a company.[13] Just sending out your résumé is another unreliable strategy. Some stunned graduates are discovering that companies are not even accepting résumés from college graduates.

Getting the Most Out of College Placement Centers

Many of the strategies and actions necessary may not be addressed by your school's career placement center. College placement centers are just as confused as the rest of the world about the amount of change taking place in the workplace, and the methods they once advocated may no longer work.

"College sends you out wearing rose-colored glasses," says a now-employed research analyst. "I could have used more information on how to get ahead, how to network, where to look for a job."[14] Another graduate who completed an arduous job search says, "In college, you learn your field, but there is no class that teaches you about résumés, job hunting, interview skills and real work situations. You have to get information from friends who've graduated, career counselors, anyone you know who hires people, and read anything you can get your hands on. You must take the initiative."[15]

Most college placement centers are working as hard as they can to come up with successful job-search strategies for today's market. They are the ones sponsoring previously unheard-of seminars like *New Ways to Find Work: Alternatives to Full Time, Finding Jobs in Government and Small Companies,* and *Relocation Job Search: How to Find a Job in Another Geographic Area.*[16] They are building these programs around the new key job-search building blocks of "packaging," "networking" and "proactive strategies."[17] Some centers are coming up with truly innovative techniques and resources. In a quest to identify positions in small companies, the University of Virginia bought a mailing list of 10,000 area firms that have 200 or less employees. Access to a new database called *Career Search* is being offered to students and alumni at some colleges, including Oberlin, Babson, Cornell and University of Miami. It is a huge directory that profiles 210,000 companies, including banks, insurers, high-tech firms and manufacturers. *Career Search* users can target companies by product or service, and then make further selections using detailed criteria including location, size, sales and commuting distance from major cities. Other schools, like San Francisco State University, have set up job phone banks with listings students and alumni can access by phone.[18]

Conduct a thorough investigation of what your placement center has to offer and use everything relevant. At the same time, look at other resources if your center doesn't include multiple job-search strategies, encourage new ways of thinking and offer some unconventional approaches.

Where Are You Going? You May Not Know Until You Get There

"My heart belongs to writing, but I found it hard to break into it just out of school, even with a journalism degree. So now I'm learning a trade I didn't even study," says Barbara Zeigler Mende, an assistant media planner in the New York office of advertising agency Kirshenbaum and Bond.[19] Actually, this type of change is pretty typical. In fact, rather than avoiding it, you should seek it out. Don't limit your career objectives in terms of what type of work you want to do. Melanie Seidner, an assistant merchandiser for BabyGap in San Francisco, says, "I majored in English, had no inkling I'd be interested in retailing, but when The Gap recruiter was on campus, I signed up because it was a company name I recognized."[20]

Even if you have very straightforward, clearly defined goals, you need to be flexible. Perhaps you majored in biology and planned on working for a company that manufactures medical equipment. But you may find that you want to more broadly redefine your goal as a position somewhere in the health care industry and open yourself up to more possibilities. Instead of working for a diagnostic equipment manufacturer, for example, you might end up in a company that owns a national chain of outpatient treatment centers that utilize diagnostic equipment.

Some educational paths and degrees seem to be more in demand than others. Employment projections indicate that graduates with technical education and majors such as chemistry and computer science will more easily find job opportunities than those in humanities or business administration. But even "soft subject" majors can benefit by keeping their options open. An English graduate should look beyond the publishing or advertising industries. A broader perspective would be to recognize that "hot" areas like health care may be good options. Health care companies hire public relations and advertising people. And there are over 800 medical and dental journals currently in publication, all of which have staffs ranging from editorial assistants to subscription and circulation managers.[21]

Think creatively to figure out where your background might apply outside the obvious choices. Don't become frustrated by having to look at alternatives. "I wish someone had told me how small my field, art education, is and how difficult it would be to get a job in it," says Wendi James.* But she didn't give up. After looking for a job in art education for a year, Wendi sought other options. She now works as a computer graphics artist, which she feels has been a good choice. Her education was relevant in qualifying her for the job, and she is earning a decent salary.[22]

Broadening Your Company Options

When targeting potential employers, don't stick to "the classics." In the past, most graduates focused on large companies. But large companies have been laying off thousands of employees. "The days when a college graduate could segue from the shelter of academia to the cocoon of a big corporation offering job security, steady promotion and an array of benefits are dwindling fast. The greatest job growth is among smaller and mid-size companies that offer risk and not a whole lot of benefits," reports the *Los Angeles Times*.[23] Dun & Bradstreet estimates that of the net 1.9 million new jobs created this year (*net* = subtracting those lost through large company cutbacks), 80 percent will be created in companies with less than 100 employees.[24]

Graduates will find advantages and disadvantages in small companies. Often, a recent graduate's enthusiasm and energy is a good fit with a smaller company's pace and spirit. New hires generally do more and learn faster than those in larger firms, hemmed in by procedures and bureaucracy. "We're growing so fast, my job description changes almost weekly," says Jim Gorka, an accounting major working for

165-employee Steris Corp., a manufacturer of medical equipment. After getting rejections from 70 large companies, Gorka called Steris and found a job in accounting. While his starting salary was less than he wanted, he was promoted from accountant to supervisor of information systems with a corresponding raise. And, rather than being "stuck in accounts receivable," he's logged experience that would haven taken years to get in a large company.[25]

On the down side, small companies are often risky because their financial stability can be fragile. But new graduates, less likely than older workers to be burdened with mortgages and families, often better tolerate the risk. Smaller companies lean towards hiring people with experience since many don't provide formal training. New hires usually need to walk in and start working, so graduates with any kind of experience in their field, including unpaid internships, need to emphasize this experience when presenting themselves to small companies.

Calling on Your Initiative, Creativity and Persistence

Applying an open-minded and flexible attitude in executing your job search will speed up the process. Identify every possible way of looking for a job and do all of them. You have no way of knowing what will work, so it's vital that you do them all.

Use every personal contact. In addition to obvious contacts like former employers and school alumni, your list should include everyone—your parent's friends, your dentist and your dry cleaner. The golden rule here is that *everyone knows someone and you don't know who knows who, so you need to ask.* Don't worry about appearing pushy. This is no time to be shy. Successful job seekers get up their courage and talk to everyone who may be useful, even if they're uncertain about results. If you talk to someone who can't or won't help you, you haven't lost anything, but if you don't ask, you may be missing a great lead.

Create ways to meet appropriate people. For example, look into trade shows and conventions in your industry and attend them. If you effectively market yourself when you get there, even a trip requiring your own travel money can pay off. Scott Wollschlager graduated from the University of Wisconsin with a degree in food service administration. Part of the $3,800 he spent on his job search included attending eight food-industry trade shows. At the shows he handed out "business cards" with a condensed résumé printed on them. His efforts resulted in landing a job with Prime Label, a company that consults to meat and poultry producers.[26]

Through trade shows, phone calls or mail, *contact companies on your own*, regardless of whether you know they are hiring. In both good and bad times, this is probably the most successful job-search technique, and the one job seekers often do the least. Many college graduates aren't even aware "cold calling" is an option. Sometimes, when I ask college grads if they are contacting companies, they respond, "You can't do that, can you?" *Yes, yes, yes—you can and you should.* Only an estimated 14 percent of all positions are advertised.[27] Networking is good, but it's next to impossible to meet someone who knows someone in every company that might be a potential employer for you. The best way to see if there might be a place for you in a given company is to contact them. (See Chapter 17, Job Search, as well as Afterword: What Do I Do Next? at the end of this book.)

Use the library. Present yourself to the librarian at the business section of the reference room and *ask for help*. You will be surprised by how much information you can get your hands on. Library resources can include chamber of commerce directories, trade journals, professional association memberships, detailed databases and more. I've had clients who made great "finds" at the library that led to jobs. Discoveries range from a membership directory of national food brokers that led to an invitation to a national trade show for a graduate in nutrition, to a directory listing all of the companies in a major high-tech, biotechnology complex, a tool that became a gold mine for a chemistry major.

It takes time and diligence to do this kind of research, but it's worth it. A public relations assistant who "searched her heart out" during her job hunt says, "You need to research a lot of companies—learn where the jobs are, what you can expect to be paid, what kind of position you might have in five to 10 years. I wish I'd read business, financial, and trade publications while I was still in school. College doesn't prepare you for how hard you really have to work [to find a job] when you get out. The competition is tough—there are so many good people."[28] Identifying an actual job opportunity and securing an interview takes work.

Some Interviewing Smarts

At last, the big moment. You finally have the chance to see and speak to someone with the potential to hire you. It's time for you to perform. This can be a scary experience—it's in person, it's important and you don't want to blow it.

Fear is normal. Everyone, regardless of how much experience they have, is nervous interviewing. Each has particular worries about how they could mess up. Most people in the workforce can relate their own interviewing nightmare experience, one they remember for the rest of their lives. Client horror stories have included the gentleman who started his interview with an unexpected, very messy sneeze and no Kleenex in sight; the woman whose interviewer was not only drunk, but offered her a sip from the bottle he had hidden in his desk; and the interviewee who confused one job interview with another one and tailored all her responses to the wrong job and wrong company.

The point is—everyone makes mistakes. College graduates are no exception. To help minimize the pitfalls, here are some special *dos* and *don'ts* that apply to anyone who may lack experience in the interviewing game. They're tips to help you do the right things, avoid the wrong things and not make any more mistakes than an experienced job seeker.

First of all, realize that the interview process starts before the actual interview. It begins when you are given an application to fill out or when you walk into the building. Everything you do can "count" for or against you.

Your interview literally begins when you enter the lobby. Don't discount the receptionist or secretary and not bother to be on your best behavior until the interviewer shows up. It *is* true that interviewers will ask receptionists how you acted or treated them. "That person was really rude" or "Well, she acted like a jerk" can eliminate you from the running no matter how well the actual interview went. People don't want to hire people who don't know how to act appropriately.

Apply the same consideration to how you sit and what you read. Don't slouch in your chair, fidget or sigh loudly if you are kept waiting. If you're interviewing with a financial services company, pass up the *People* magazine and pick up the issue of *BusinessWeek* instead. What magazine you read before your interview can make a difference, however small, when it is one of the many things being considered in the decision process. One human resources interviewer with a major retail chain always peeks into the lobby to look at the candidate before she comes out to introduce herself. She says she pays attention to what she sees. "The applicant who looks alert, doesn't slouch, maybe examines materials on the bulletin board or chats with the receptionist—she already has some pluses."[29]

When you do enter that lobby, always be appropriately dressed. You should be in interview attire, even if you are just dropping off an application at the reception desk. Showing up in jeans for this kind of errand is not appropriate and could hurt your chances. It's not worth the risk.

Your communication skills—speaking, listening and writing—count here. "So many personnel managers tell me job applicants don't know how to speak—or listen," says Dean Victor R. Lindquist at Northwestern University. "Poor oral communication/presentation skills" was the second biggest turnoff cited by human resource interviewers in the Northwestern University study.[30]

Keep in mind that writing includes content and *penmanship*. Before you even touch an application with your pen, think about your handwriting. Do you put curlicues over your "i's?" Is a "happy face" part of your signature? If you do anything like this, *stop doing it.* It's important to communicate with grown-up handwriting, which is quite different from messages written in someone's yearbook, or stick-on notes left on the refrigerator for your roommate.

Don't forget that communicating includes *listening.* While every interview has its own rhythm and pace, be sure you listen to your interviewer so that you make appropriate responses rather than ramble on in a non-stop, unappreciated filibuster and blow the interview.

Pay attention to how you speak. Don't be too casual, even if the person interviewing you is young. Take the safer and more appropriate approach, such as, "Hello. It's good to meet you," rather than "Hi!"

Be careful about using slang words and expressions. Make a conscious effort not to use the word "like." "So, I am like really interested in this job" is a no-no. And don't make statements with the same intonation as questions: "I graduated in June? With a degree in journalism?" The information may be correct, but the tone is wrong. You are telling the interviewer this information, not asking him or her to confirm it. A business situation demands that you speak appropriately. "In the real world, you have to know how to conduct real conversations with people at all levels—there's a whole different etiquette for the president of your company than for your roommate," says a recently employed graduate.[31]

Be sure that your verbal and non-verbal communication match. Let's say you are in an interview and the person interviewing you asks if you are willing to relocate. You're not, but you don't want to tell the interviewer, so you say, "Yes," but avert your eyes and shift around in your chair.

Don't send these kinds of mixed messages. A better response would be to say that it would depend upon the specific position.

During the interview, try to avoid clichéd responses. One of the most common is saying you "want to work with people." This has become a meaningless phrase. Virtually everyone works with people. Even laboratory biologists interact with people in addition to mice or bacteria. You'll do much better if you can identify the ways you want to work with people, says Beth Gottlieb, director of the Career Placement Center at Hobart and William Smith Colleges in New York. "If you're applying for a banking job, for instance, you could say, 'I'd like to assist clients with their financial questions.'"[32]

Ask the right questions. It *is* important to ask questions in an interview, rather than just passively answer them. Not having questions to ask looks like you either don't care or aren't sharp enough to think of any. Many books and materials offer helpful suggestions of questions to ask. (See Afterword and Suggested Reading sections.) Be sure that the questions you ask are appropriate and that you understand them, cautions Patty Doyle, a recruiter for a major paper company. "I've had people ask, 'Why did your profit margin increase by three percent?'—but their eyes are glazed because they have no idea what the question means."[33] This will hurt, not help.

Experience Counts

Realize that when employers interview graduates, they are looking for people who understand the "real world." The best way to show you understand the real world is to have job experience you can point to. *Any* job experience helps. Being a lab assistant or a waiter can be of equal benefit. If you are looking for a job in a science-related industry, then being a lab assistant is good—it proves you have some experience, knowledge and competence in your chosen area. But if you worked as a waiter throughout school, it can be positive in a different, but just as important, way. It shows you know how to handle more than one thing—work and school—at a time. If you've survived waiting on people in food establishments, you probably learned to get along with people, have decent communication skills and can work under stress.

Too often, students will discount work they have done during school, saying, "Oh, I was just a salesperson during Christmas" or "I just bagged groceries during the summer. No one is going to care about that." Wrong. *Just the fact that you worked makes a difference.* It means you understand the concept of holding a job, of showing up, carrying out responsibilities and juggling priorities in your life. Entering the full-time workforce with any work experience is always preferable to having none. "Most employers want students to have some work experience, some kind of experience besides a degree," says Bruce Riesenberg, associate director of Career Planning and Placement at the University of California at Irvine.[34] It shows you have "cut your teeth" in the work world as well as in the classroom. Also, a large percentage of your competition is likely to have job experience acquired while in school.

Remember that work experience isn't restricted to work you were paid for. Volunteer and unpaid internships are just as important as paid positions. Actually, sometimes they can be more important because they often show experience in an area actually related to your work objective.

Reviewing Your Options

Suppose, after considerable effort, you can't find a full-time, "normal" job. There are alternatives.

One alternative to burger-flipping at the local fast food parlor is to **work part time** or **take temporary jobs.** Part-time work or temping allows you to gain experience and develop and sharpen your skills, which is particularly useful if you didn't work much or at all during college. It also helps you network and often can be a foot in the door. Temporary or part-time jobs still turn into full-time opportunities for some people, either in the work they were hired to do or in another function or department they were exposed to while there. Also, part-time or temporary work doesn't necessarily have to be clerical. Companies are hiring part-time and temporary employees in professional capacities, such as computer programming, public relations and engineering. (See Chapter 8, Exploring New Options.)

Another option is to **work as a volunteer.** In today's tight job market, an increasing number of graduates are looking at volunteerism as a logical way of entering the workplace. Applications to programs like Volunteers in Service to America (VISTA), the Peace Corps and Teach for America are way up. In January of 1992, the Peace Corps' Washington, D.C., telephone lines were jammed with 900 inquiries a day, up from 150 to 200 a day the year before. The percentage of students in VISTA has risen from 11 to 15 percent of the total number of volunteers.[35]

Some believe this surge to volunteer isn't motivated solely by the tight job market, but that "idealism" is a contributing factor. "College students are a lot more idealistic than the media gives them credit for," says Wendy Kopp, the founder of Teach for America.[36] Whatever the reasons, interest is definitely on the rise. New programs like *Public Allies: The National Center for Careers in Public Life* are springing up. Established programs, like the Peace Corps, which plans to create 250 to 500 field positions in the Commonwealth of Independent States (formerly the Soviet Union), are expanding.[37] The demand for recruits and the increase in student interest in VISTA has enabled the program to win congressional funding to hire nine college campus recruiters.[38]

The volunteer experience can be rewarding on a personal level. VISTA, considered a domestic Peace Corps, deals with homelessness, drug abuse, hunger and unemployment in the United States. Volunteers enlist for a year. They are paid about $610 monthly and receive a supplemental $95 per month for each month of service upon completion of their commitment. While the pay for public service jobs is low, the experience can be invaluable and personally satisfying. Marty Siewert, a graduate from Northwestern University, who works at the Los Angeles Free Clinic, says, ". . . every day, you feel like you have a chance to make a difference. You don't get that with many jobs."[39]

Teach for America is the brainchild of a creative and entrepreneurial college student. Wendy Kopp conceived the idea for the program in her senior thesis and founded it in 1990.[40] It is a privately funded, non-profit organization that puts people without teaching degrees through a two-month training program and then places them into two-year teaching positions in needy urban and rural areas. Ninety percent of the teachers placed through the program in 1991 were recent college graduates. The pay is decent. Teach for America teachers receive the going rate for the local school where they teach, which can range from a low of $15,000 in Arkansas to a high of $29,000 in Los Angeles.[41]

If public service doesn't attract you, you can pick up valuable work experience by **being an intern.** Internships are an option even if you've already graduated. There are two ways to go about becoming an intern. One is to apply to companies that have established internship positions. The other way is to create your own internship by contacting companies and offering your services for a specified period of time, even a week, for a particular project. (Self-initiated internships are sometimes called *externships.*)

Creating an internship takes some initiative and persistence. It means calling companies and explaining what you want to do and what you have to offer. Some companies, particularly smaller ones, may even be flattered and appreciative of your interest. Small companies are also a good bet because they are likely to be approached by fewer job hunters, and you often get to do more in a small company due to the small staff size.

However you get them, internships are worth it. Even if you aren't paid, you are gaining experience and a track record in an area related to your work objective; and presuming you do a good job, you'll also get references and contacts. Internships can make a difference. Maury Hanigan, who consults to General Electric, Xerox and Unilever on-campus recruiting, says that among engineering majors who had held summer internships, 76 percent received job offers at graduation. "Internships are becoming more and more important," says Hanigan. "That's where students learn the soft skills of working in a corporate environment."[42]

Trying on Entrepreneurship

Some graduates, finding the traditional job market dried up, are deciding that starting their own venture is worth the risk. While only a few graduates create their own businesses, those that do find the advantages worthwhile. Thomas Madonia started Atlanta Multigraphics, a computer animation and graphic service, right out of school. For him, entrepreneurship was a logical move. "I'm single, 23-years old, and I don't have a family to support," he says. "And there was no way to make less money than I was while being unemployed."[43]

If this appeals to you as well, the odds for success are better if your business is based on something you know, doesn't require a lot of start-up funding and will produce results quickly so you can remain in business until you see a profit. William Haeberle, president of the National Entrepreneurship Foundation, an advisory group for young entrepreneurs, and professor emeritus of management at Indiana University's business school, says, "The risk of a business goes down substantially for [young people] if they go into something they were doing in school or beforehand, including a summer job or even a hobby."[44] (See Chapter 9, Going On Your Own.)

The Graduate-School Alternative

Another option to full-time employment is to continue your education and go on to graduate school, the frequent choice of many who don't know what else to do. "A lot of [my friends] are just going to graduate school because the market isn't ready for this many engineers," says a graduate with a B.A. in electrical engineering.[45] Over 81 percent of graduating college students surveyed by employment consultants Right Associates in 1991 said they planned to pursue advanced degrees. This was up from 77 percent in 1990. When listing factors they thought would help them get better jobs, college students ranked "improved education" as third in importance, up from eighth place in previous studies.[46]

If you do decide to continue your education, select your advanced studies carefully. Focus on graduate work that will help make you marketable. Be aware that if continuing school means going into debt, you will have to deal with this obligation down the line in a paying job. And realize that some graduate schools prefer that you have some work experience. Jay Halfond, associate dean of Northwestern University's business school, says their ideal MBA candidate is 25 years old with three years of work experience. "The more solid the experience, the stronger the application," says Halfond.[47] Before signing up for graduate school, think through the implications and outcomes carefully. You may want to opt for finding some kind of job experience, rather than using graduate school as a time killer.

Making It Happen

Don't let a difficult job market defeat you. If you learn how to effectively look for a job and market yourself, you will succeed. You can improve your odds by using up-to-date job-search methods. Keep the faith—hold tight to the belief that you will get employed, even if the obstacles seem daunting. And be persistent. "It isn't aptitude, but attitude that gives you altitude," says one successful job seeker.[48] There is a great deal of truth in this statement.

---

* *Name and some details have been changed.*

11.

DEFENSE-INDUSTRY WORKERS

Assessing the Situation

The recession of the early 1990s and the massive cuts in defense spending have had a particularly heavy impact on the defense industry. A 1993 study by the Department of Labor estimates that an additional 1.9 million defense-related positions will be cut by 1997, with 1.2 million of these jobs being in the private sector.[1] While the effects of these cuts on the overall U.S. economy are often debated, these reductions will have an enormous impact on certain local economies and job markets in geographic areas where defense contractors are clustered. This is especially true in the 10 states that account for 59 percent of the Pentagon's procurement: California, Texas, New York, Virginia, Massachusetts, Ohio, Pennsylvania, Florida, Connecticut and New Jersey.[2]

People in the defense industry must often cope with more than the usual fears and problems experienced by other unemployed or job-insecure workers. The fact that they are part of an industrywide problem has made finding similar work more difficult. In the past, when one company within an industry cut back, its displaced employees were rehired by similar employers. Today, the across-the-board nature of defense layoffs is leaving no safe harbors or sanctuaries. Says one aerospace assembly worker, ". . . Before, if you got laid off at one place, somebody else had a big contract. Now if you get laid off, there's nowhere to go."[3]

Many unemployed defense workers who had been with the same employer for a long time have been taken by surprise. A quality engineer laid off from the space shuttle program, says, "It was a big shock. . . . I [had been] nominated the engineer of the year at Rockwell and had my picture in the newspaper. I thought I could have completed my career at Rockwell."[4]

Those hired 15 or 20 years ago may not have had to cope with the job market in a long time. For them, it's like suddenly being in a new country and not knowing the language. And it's natural to feel unprepared and resentful. Duplicating their former work status, salary and perks may be tough. Experienced defense workers are used to being paid pretty well and having generous insurance and benefits packages. These high salaries and ample benefits can be hard to match.

Another difficulty is that defense work is often very specialized, with workers developing skills and knowledge that aren't generally utilized in other industries. This specialization can affect almost everyone, from scientists to mechanics to contract administrators.

Finding the Bright Side

Many individuals and companies are convinced the tremendous talent and experience pool of the defense industry now being available to other industries and technologies will help boost the economy as well as the country. In fact, some believe that the high-tech talents sequestered in the defense industry may be better used outside of it. "Lots of people feel that too many good minds have been wasted on weapons," says Jay Stowskly, an analyst at Berkeley Roundtable on the International Economy.[5] In the late 1960s and early 1970s such a transfer of brain power happened when thousands of aerospace workers lost their jobs as the Apollo space program and the Vietnam War wound down, and the nuclear power industry slowed. Many of these workers were able to become part of the semiconductor industry that exploded the following decade.[6]

Whether you buy into this premise or not, if you are a former defense industry employee, you need to recognize that you must change any negative thinking you may be harboring and promptly adopt the "brain power availability" positive attitude. This will greatly help you make your next career move, whether it means going with a defense-related business, moving into a commercial arena, transitioning your skills into a totally different industry or starting your own venture. All require creative positive thinking, persistence and persuasion.

Defense-Conversion Considerations

Opportunities for employment are emerging as part of the "defense-conversion" movement. There are jobs to be had with companies making a switch from defense to commercial products and services. Some focus on *non-military* projects, but continue to work with the government, where they can not only use their technologies in different applications, but have the advantage of knowing how to work with the government as their client. "We're leveraging our defense technology and expertise into other areas," says Richard A. Linder, Westinghouse Electric's president,[7] whose company is designing air-traffic-control systems and bus-tracking systems for Baltimore, Milwaukee and Denver. Lockheed Corporation is building satellites to locate drivers with unpaid parking tickets for the City of Los Angeles.[8] Rockwell, Hughes Aircraft Co., Lockheed and other defense companies are bidding on projects created by the $700 million allocated to develop high-tech highways and vehicles as a result of the passage of the federal Intermodal Surface Transportation Efficiency Act in 1991.[9] Northrop Corporation in Southern California is also getting into technology conversion projects focusing on the transportation industry. It is currently involved in the design and development of an advanced bus and has joined with a Canadian rail company to develop a proposal for the Los Angeles Metro Rail System. Non-military government work like this can be a lucrative area that preserves and creates jobs. TRW, which began focusing on this kind of work in 1987, has since doubled revenues in non-defense government contracts to $500 million.[10]

Other companies to seek out are those leaving or expanding out from the government sector and pursuing commercial clients. Since 1991, over half of 148 defense contractors have begun marketing commercial products based on defense technology, according to a study conducted by the consulting firm Winbridge Group.[11]

The burgeoning health care industry is a logical place for the transfer of some defense technologies. Health care technology is similar to aerospace in that it demands the same exacting quality standards, precision, advanced engineering and detailed paper trail. FHM Corp. in Irvine, California, has shifted from manufacturing aerospace components to medical devices. The same General Dynamics division that made the driving coupling for the Atlas Rocket is now making parts used in blood-processing machines. Michael Williamson, who once designed cruise missile guidance systems, currently designs computerized drug-dispensing machines at a new, growing firm called Pyxis in San Diego, California.[12]

The automotive industry is another sector that often meshes well with defense, as it proactively assesses how defense-initiated technologies can be used in its own companies. Rockwell Corporation, for example, has an automotive engineering division working on reshaping car roofs to reduce noise during travel, using the same computational fluid-dynamics technology utilized to modify the NASA space shuttle design. Ford, Chrysler and Honda are all interested in using U.S. Army-developed technology to mount miniature radar transceivers into rearview mirrors in automobiles. Other opportunities are opening up with automakers such as General Motors, Ford and Chrysler Corp., who are looking into outsourcing functions that can be done less expensively by other companies, as part of their efforts to reduce costs and be more competitive. This outsourcing, says David Cole, an auto-industry expert at the University of Michigan, creates opportunities for suppliers like defense companies who have advanced technology and the ability to integrate complex systems. Rockwell, for example, has set a goal to sell $3 billion in auto parts by 1996, up from its current $2.4 billion, sales which will account for 21 percent of annual revenue.[13]

In addition to the most likely markets, there are a number of other industries that offer potential to defense contractors. Hughes Aircraft Co. is **targeting the entertainment and telecommunications industries as conversion markets**. Hughes wants to use its expertise in satellite communications to provide movies, sports and other television programming by satellite to both cable subscribers and some of the 12 million U.S. households out of reach of cable TV. It is also looking into selling cellular-phone systems to developing regions that cannot afford the expensive infrastructure of conventional phone networks, as well as marketing its own cellular phones domestically.[14]

Starting Your Own Venture

Some former defense workers are switching from defense to commercial industries by starting their own companies either alone or in partnership with others. The key here is to have a niche market to focus on. If, as a former defense worker, you feel you have a product to sell to a carefully defined market, you may want to consider starting your own business. However, before latching on to this idea, it's important to carefully evaluate what it takes to start and successfully operate a new business, since the same success and failure factors apply to aerospace spinoffs as they do to any start-up venture. (See Chapter 9, Going On Your Own.)

There have been some notable successes with start-up companies and consulting roles. For example, Bruce Morse, who once programmed computerized maps for the U.S. Navy at Hughes Aircraft, now consults with city governments to design systems where city planners and utilities workers can "push a button" and locate water and power lines. In Sunny-vale, California, scientists from Rockwell, TRW and Stanford University formed a business targeting the development of new medical diagnostic equipment, using their superconduc-tor experience.[15] Kwang-I Yu, a promising young scientist for-merly at TRW Corp., has started Paracel Inc. to manufacture a revolutionary, high-speed data-search device based on a computer chip he invented.[16]

Taking a New Perspective

Not all defense companies or employees can make a suc-cessful transition into commercial markets. The conversion from defense to commercial markets may only balance 25 percent to 30 percent of defense work losses, predicts Sal Monaco, a consultant with forecaster DRI/McGraw-Hill.[17] Companies and workers who do make the change success-fully are creative, innovative and open-minded. Carol D. Campbell, with Hughes Aircraft's Missile Systems Co., was given the job of finding new commercial markets for her company's products. After much research, she realized that Hughes' missile-targeting technology could be used to deci-pher sloppy handwriting. This discovery led to Hughes' suc-cessful competition against IBM, Eastman Kodak and AT&T with the winning of a major "character-recognition" contract with the U.S. Postal Service, one that could grow to $100 million in revenues.[18]

Creativity—seeing new ways to apply technology— is a key factor to succeeding, as are flexibility and a posi-tive attitude toward change. There are differences in val-ues, expectations and business practices in non-defense industries. To make the transition, you must abandon old mind-sets and take on these differences as assets rather than liabilities.

One of the key challenges is *adjusting to the different de-mands of non-defense customers*. Unlike the Department of Defense (DOD), commercial customers often demand fast pro-duction and turnaround while requiring fewer administrative procedures and less documentation. Selling a can of chili con carne, which consists of beans, water and ground beef, to the DOD can mean filling out 35 pages of specifications, notes Daniel Burton of the Private Council on Competitiveness. Private industry, on the other hand, won't require the 35 pages, but needs the product quickly to compete with other chili makers.[19] Ted Lesster, a propulsion expert from Westinghouse, headed a team that won a contract to design a powertrain for Chrysler Corp.'s electronic minivan. Realizing the differences in urgency and expectations held by their new client, Lesster's team made some radical departures from defense-industry practices by discarding formal design review procedures and letting a team of 15 engineers manage its own schedule. Such successful changes allowed them to build a prototype in six months, while a similar project on a defense schedule would have taken twice as long. They got the message and delivered. "In the commercial world," says Lesster, "you have to prove your worth with hardware, not paper ideas."[20]

Making the switch to non-defense-industry product specifications, performance expectations and marketing techniques can require an adjustment in thinking. Richard Campbell, president of Westinghouse Security Systems, says it was hard to move employees from manufacturing military radars to home burglar alarms. "We had to get people adjusted to the idea this thing doesn't have to be able to fall off an 80-story building or survive minus 40 degrees Celsius," says Campbell.[21]

The defense industry does not market its products within the traditional private-sector definition of marketing. "In the defense world, you're notified of bids, you negotiate a long-term relationship and you don't go knocking on doors and say, 'Here's our brochure,'" states Bruce Andrews, who was president of now-defunct UNC Naval Products.[22] Defense products are carefully detailed in DOD specifications. By contrast, in the commercial world, companies usually need to do their own extensive market research and create the specifications and plans for the client, rather than having them supplied by the client. Differences like these have resulted in defense contractors making reactive marketing bids as opposed to the proactive marketing moves required in the commercial sector.

To be successful in the commercial marketplace, companies and employees need to be adaptive. Rockwell's successful penetration of the automotive market is due largely to the tremendous changes the company made to compete in this market. Rockwell had to break with tradition and do things differently, such as implementing self-managed work teams, according to Kent Black, who oversees several Rockwell businesses that include an auto-related network of 56 plants in 17 countries employing over 17,000 workers.[23]

Making career moves outside of the defense-industry envelope demands initiative and the ability to think and act beyond the norms and constraints of your previous occupation and industry. It requires a change in thinking, such as moving your mental focus from carrying out detailed plans to initiating them from scratch.

Developing a Plan of Attack

1. **Conduct a personal "skills and experience assessment" to determine what your marketable talents are.** First, carefully analyze your background to determine your basic skills and areas of expertise. Then look at other industries and occupations to see how your talents can "transfer" to other areas. *Think of yourself as a "product" and other industries or occupations as "markets" that you are targeting and selling your "product" to.* (See Afterword and Suggested Reading sections for skills assessments resources.)

2. **Explore the possibility of switching from defense to commercial areas using your transferable skills.** Thoroughly research your former employer to see if defense conversion is being planned and if there is a part for you in one of the projects. If you worked for a large company, explore *all*

divisions of the company, not just the one you worked in.

If your company is making the switch, find out if it is receiving diversification assistance. Some states, like New York, Connecticut and Virginia, have created diversification programs that include how-to workshops and financial aid for companies. Other states are trying to pass legislation to help defense-industry contractors enter new fields. If your company is involved in these types of programs, you should thoroughly explore them and pursue any job opportunities.

3. **Take advantage of *any and all* programs offered by your employer, industry, or your local, state or federal government.** These can include classic outplacement services (job-search counseling), company-sponsored entrepreneurial training or industry-sponsored job fairs. Through the 1992 Defense Conversion Act, Congress has appropriated $951 million to help displaced defense-industry workers. Some of these funds go to regional development schemes, like revolving loans for small businesses, but $716 million is earmarked for "personal assistance programs" to provide job counseling, retraining and temporary health insurance to former military or civilians laid off by the DOD or defense contractors.[24]

4. **Network with former employees.** If they have started their own venture, see if there is a place for you. If they haven't, and you have synergistic talents and experience, talk to them about getting something going. If this interests you, there are some venture capital firms specializing in defense-conversion funding. Get busy and try to find them.

5. **Look into temporary opportunities.** Some commercial employers are hiring on a temporary, project basis. This can be a good way to build your own conversion skills and gain experience on the commercial side. Motorola Inc.'s Advanced Microcontroller Division has hired dozens of temporary defense engineers for software development in areas like neural networks and fuzzy logic.

6. **If you're a risk-taker, look into starting your own venture.** This can include defense-related areas, defense-conversion ideas or businesses totally unrelated to the defense industry. A lot of training is available to former defense workers contemplating starting their own businesses. In California, there are about 25 entrepreneurial training centers sponsored by private and public groups, including the Greater San Diego Chamber of Commerce. Training includes customer identification, competitive analysis, budgeting and finances, management techniques, marketing and manufacturing.[25] (See Chapter 9, Going On Your Own.)

Like any other former corporate employee starting his or her own business, plan on facing enormous changes. "The thing about aerospace was that I was so used to being taken care of," says Jarl Neslon, who started his own pool cleaning business after being laid off three times since 1982. "It's a major shock to be out in the real world. But I'll make a success of my business. I love being my own boss, calling my own shots."[26]

Positively Coping With Change

Refreshing your perspective and attitudes is vital if you want to make the transition. So is taking control. Harry Luettchau, who was laid off after 10 years at TRW and now owns a glass and mirror business, candidly states, "Getting laid off was traumatic. It was a blast in the ass. I had three choices: stew in my brew, put on a suit and tie and bang my head against the wall trying to compete, or create my own destiny."[27] Now is the time to choose to move forward and not "stew in your brew."

12. DISABLED WORKERS

P eople with disabilities comprise the fastest-growing minority in the workplace. Currently, an estimated 16 percent of the total population, or 43 million people, have some sort of disability.[1] Of these, 20 million are of working age (16 to 64 years old).[2]

By 2010, the number of people with disabilities is predicted to grow, with 70 percent of the population having some kind of disability during their lives.[3] Disabilities, as defined under the 1990 Americans with Disabilities Act (ADA), are physical or mental impairments that substantially limit a major life activity. These can include: vision, hearing or speech impairments, emotional disturbance and mental illness, seizure disorders, mental retardation, learning disabilities, and orthopedic and neuromotor disabilities. The Act also specifies certain serious health impairments, such as diabetes, heart or lung disease, cancer, asthma, cystic fibrosis, Crohn's disease, hepatitis B carriers, HIV infection, alcoholism and drug addiction, to name a few.[4]

Approaching the Job Search

As with anyone looking for a job or seeking career advancement, the disabled person must present his or her capabilities in a positive light and put considerable effort into the task. Success is dependent on the quality of effort put forth and on the attitude of the job seeker. "Someone recovering from a disability . . . has often had to survive in the system by depending on, and accentuating, their *lack* of ability in order to receive funds for survival," says Miriam Whitfield, program director with Social Vocational Services in Los Angeles. "It takes a major mental adjustment to stop relying on your *inabilities* for your success and start exercising those *abilities* you've had buried for so long."[5]

Disabled people are the same as anyone applying for a job, says Barbara Haney, director of community resources for Employ America, a private, non-profit agency in California. "Some go in with a lot of confidence, feeling they will succeed, and others feel deflated, defeated and discouraged. It depends on the personality, moxie and the self-confidence level of the person and their family and support systems," adds Haney.[6]

All of your job-search strategies, from résumés to interviews to references, need to accentuate your abilities and present a positive attitude. Persons with disabilities can get the job done; they are "equal to the task," asserts the Du Pont Company.[7] But they must be assertive in their approach.

Changing Attitudes

"The most important barriers to the employment of disabled people are attitudinal barriers," says Gallaudet University (for the hearing-impaired) president Dr. I. King. "Often we're judged unable to do something before we're given an opportunity to try."[8] Disabled job seekers and workers must do their part to focus employers on the positive aspects of their place in the workforce.

In the past, many people didn't see how the disabled could be a useful part of the workforce. But these attitudes are improving. In a 1991 survey, 80 percent of those interviewed felt that people with disabilities had unused potential to contribute to society, and similar numbers felt it would be a "boost to the nation" if more disabled people were employed. John

Kemp, 42-year-old executive director of United Cerebral Palsy Association, who, having been born without arms or legs, walks with prosthetics, says that significant improvements have been made in the last 15 or 20 years, ". . . not only in the accessibility of many facilities [for the disabled], . . . but also in people's attitudes. I think we're starting to see an empathy or understanding by more people."[9]

Incentives to Employers

Employers are more motivated to employ disabled people today than in the past. A variety of national programs are available that provide incentives for employers hiring disabled workers:

- Employee leasing programs allow companies to economically increase their workforce without adding to their head count. The leasing agency hires, trains, pays and provides health care coverage for the employee and the hiring business pays a fee for leasing the new employee.

- There are also supported employment programs, which provide training and an on-the-job coach for any disabled worker hired by a company through the program.

- Companies can apply for a Targeted Job Tax Credit, which financially compensates companies employing disabled people.

- Other incentives may be offered through federal or state-sponsored programs.

Community Hospital of Central California developed its own innovative program that has saved the hospital $900,000 in workers' compensation claims and reduced lost-time claims by 50 percent.[10] The program allows injured employees to make changes in their workload and stay on the job, keeping them salaried and productive, rather than relegated to long-term disability benefits.

In addition to financial incentives, employers are finding disabled workers to be a good investment, ranking among

the hardest working, highest performing and most depend-
able. Often they come from training programs that are equal
to or better than those of non-disabled workers. Alys
Klingenberg, project director for New York State Data Processing for Disabled People, says that employers consider its
students as well prepared as any non-disabled students produced by a co-op program.[11] "Most employers say the bottom line is a win/win situation for the business and the person
with a disability," states Employ America's Haney.[12]

Fair Practices and Accommodations Under the ADA

In 1990, Congress passed the Americans with Disabilities Act (ADA) which requires employers to accommodate the
special needs of the disabled. Under the employment provi-
sions of this Act, businesses with 25 employees or more had
to make "reasonable accommodation" by 1992 to recruit and
employ qualified applicants and employees with physical,
mental or learning disabilities. Companies with more than
15 employees but less than 25 must comply by mid-1994.[13]
Reasonable accommodations on the job can include wheelchair access, equipment such as large-print computer
screens, flexible scheduling, job sharing or many other possible accommodations depending on an employee's disability. Businesses are protected, however, by not having to
provide "reasonable accommodations" if they will cause the
employer "undue hardship."

Ultimately, the Act will affect the employment practices of
over 600,000 companies across the country. "The ADA is really at the forefront of social policy in this country," says Alan
A. Reich, president of the National Organization on Disability. "It's identifying and bringing into the mainstream a segment of the population who previously had never been thought
about as a group, and whose potential has never been recognized."[14]

ADA is not a quota or affirmative action statute, explains
Jonathan Mook, lawyer and author of a new ADA litigation
guide. "It's a totally interactive process between people with

disabilities, employers and employees."[15] Unlike an "entitle-ment" program that establishes quotas or mandates employ-ers to hire, promote or retain workers, the ADA prohibits job discrimination against qualified people with disabilities by stating they must be treated the same way the non-disabled are treated.

Employment applications, for example, must be read to blind applicants and their responses recorded. Prior to a job offer, applicants cannot be questioned about their medical history, work absenteeism due to illness, prescription drug use, past alcohol or substance abuse, or prior workers' com-pensation claims. These questions can be asked after the ac-ceptance of a job offer, but only if they are asked of all employees. Likewise, medical exams cannot be required un-less they are required for all applicants, and an employment offer cannot be withdrawn based on the outcome of a medi-cal exam.

Checking Outside Resources

Companies that don't have in-house programs to recruit disabled workers are finding there is a tremendous network of organizations that can help them. Virtually all of the ma-jor disability organizations have job-matching services. The American Council for the Blind connects employers with dis-abled professionals in 21 specialty fields. The National Asso-ciation for the Deaf, the Epilepsy Foundation of America and the National Amputation Foundation have similar programs, as do many other organizations.[16]

People with disabilities need to be aware of resources avail-able to them as well. Many organizations assist in job train-ing, placement and protection of their rights in the workplace. Government and private agencies and organizations exist for people with every manner of disability, including deafness and hearing impairments, blindness and visual impairments, cognitive and developmental disabilities, psychiatric labels and physical disabilities. These, along with other disability-advocacy groups in both the public and private sectors, actively seek out companies to inform them of the benefits of employing the disabled.

If you are not familiar with resources in your area, or want to see what else is available, a good place to start your information search is with the Job Accommodation Network (800-232-9675), the President's Committee on Employment of People with Disabilities (202-376-6200) or the Equal Employment Opportunity Commission (800-669-3362).[17]

At the state level you should contact the Governor's Commission for Employment of Persons with Disabilities. You can also tap into assistance provided by the Employment Development Department (EDD) or local employment office which offers state-run rehabilitation programs to train and place disabled workers. Check into regional sources, too. Mainstream, Inc., in Washington, D.C. (800-933-3474), provides services at the regional level. In addition, the Training Resource Network in St. Augustine, Florida (904-823-9800), publishes "Supported Employment InfoLines," a good source of current information on jobs, training and technology. Numerous non-profit agencies exist as support groups for employment of persons with disabilities.[18] New York-based Just One Break, Inc. (J.O.B.) is exclusively devoted to placing qualified disabled workers in competitive employment (212-725-2500).[19]

Eastman Kodak has hired excellent employees from the New York State Data Processing for Disabled People program. Texas Commerce Bank teamed up with the Texas Rehabilitation Commission and the Houston Business Advisory Council to form Project Independence, through which the bank has successfully hired a number of computer programmers with disabilities.[20]

Some companies, like AT&T and J.C. Penney, have worked directly with local community resources to recruit the disabled. Others work with educational and professional organizations. The U.S. Army Aberdeen Proving Group has consistently won awards for its recruitment efforts through

Gallaudet University (for the hearing-impaired) and the National Technical Institute for the Deaf.[21]

Taking Advantage of Corporate Programs

Companies' efforts to employ the disabled include developing in-house programs, working with outside organizations and educational institutions, and creating programs to retain their own workers who become disabled during their employment.

Marriott Corporation established its own non-profit organization to promote the hiring and training of disabled workers, and employs over 8,000 people with disabilities.[21] National Medical Enterprises, a worldwide organization, has developed a disabilities hiring program which they now market to other companies. American Express Co. teamed up with the National Center for Disability Services and established "Giving Us The Tools," a training program for human resources professionals on the recruitment and hiring of the disabled.[23]

Companies are finding that many changes in hiring practices can be easy and inexpensive. For example, Du Pont, a pacesetter in hiring the disabled, changed its standard job-offer letter. The company used to ask all new hires to report for work with their driver's license as ID. "That doesn't make sense. We could hire somebody who's either epileptic or has a vision impairment and doesn't drive," says Louise Perna, coordinator of Du Pont's disabilities program. The company now allows new hires to bring in any sort of photo ID.[24]

Looking Into New Technologies

Adaptive technology has become a major contributing force in increasing employment of the disabled. In a survey by the American Foundation for the Blind, 83 percent of visually impaired respondents who used computer-based adaptive technology were employed, most full time, as compared to 30 percent of the overall working-age population of visually impaired people.[25]

It is important to keep abreast of advancements in adaptive technology which can expand your capabilities. Many universities have technology centers which provide training and access to the latest in computer-assistive technology, or you can call your Regional Disability and Business Technical Assistance Center (800-949-4232).

The computer and electronics industry has led the field in providing and encouraging the development of adaptive technologies. For example:

- The Electronic Industries Association, based in Washington, D.C., established an assistive devices division in 1988.

- In 1989, Digital Equipment Corporation established the Assistive Technology Group to form partnerships with non-profit organizations and develop advanced technologies for other companies with product lines dedicated to people with disabilities.

- Xerox established a Customized Application Services Group in response to demands from its sales force to modify its equipment to meet the needs of disabled customers.

- AT&T, IBM and Apple offer a multitude of assistive devices for use of their equipment by the disabled. Apple's "Headmaster," for example, is a combination headset that allows people with no muscle control below the neck to use their computer via a "sip and puff" tube operated by mouth.[26]

Company Accommodations Boost Employment

Some companies employ disabled workers as telecommuters, working at home. American Express Company's Project Homebound allows people to do word processing from their home with company-provided equipment. Disabled telecommuters make up a significant part of the workforce for market research organizations such as Louis Harris and Associates and The Gallup Organization.[27]

Often, accommodations take place on-site in the form of job sharing. Marriott Corp., for instance, allows its workers with hearing impairments to trade phone responsibilities for paperwork tasks with non-hearing-impaired workers.[28]

Social Vocational Services' Miriam Whitfield says she's found that one of the main barriers to employing the disabled is that **employers are afraid of getting stuck with major expenses in job and workplace adjustments, but typically 80 percent end up costing less than $100.**[29]

Nationally, initial accommodation expenditures are estimated at $16 million by the private sector and $25 million by the government for EEOC enforcement.[30] To help defray these costs, tax credits and deductions are available to employers. But estimates show the cost is well worth it. Expenses are expected to be offset by a $164 million increase in productivity and a savings of $222 million resulting from decreased government support and gained income taxes from disabled workers previously not in the workforce.[31] Not to mention the addition of untapped talents to the workplace.

John Yeh is deaf. He earned his undergraduate degree at Gallaudet University and a master's in computer science from the University of Maryland. Yeh, a former computer programmer who had trouble getting hired by companies, is the founder and owner of Integrated Microcomputer Systems, which, today, has revenues of over $34 million. Yeh's determination showed that disabled workers have a useful role in business. "I want the business world to understand that disabled people can perform well if given the opportunity," he says.[32]

13.

*T*HE
MILITARY

The current and projected reductions in defense spend-ing are estimated to eliminate about 800,000 military-service jobs by 1997. Since 1989, 300,000 military person-nel have flooded the job market, and this trend will most likely continue.[1] Rather than outright cutbacks, the military hopes that most of these reductions can be accomplished through attrition—regular retirement, early retirement, and even by unprecedented yearly payment or lump-sum incentives to dis-courage re-enlistment of younger personnel who wouldn't nor-mally qualify for any kind of retirement income.

Making the Transition

While it's certainly a shock for any person suddenly thrust into the job market after years of secure employment with a single employer, for people leaving the military, the impact can be tremendous, especially if they hadn't planned to leave. The military is a much different kind of employer than the rest of the work world in our country. Traditionally, it has been all-encompassing and exceeds the role of almost all pri-vate sector employers by furnishing services and benefits for its employees and their families in virtually all aspects of their lives. Housing and medical care are provided, consumer household items are purchased at discounts in commissar-ies, and children often attend military-base schools. Social and community life is also "provided" in the sense that most friendships and social activities take place with other people and families in the military.

While it may give more, the military also asks more of its people. ". . . [it] impose[s] demands on our people beyond anything the commercial sector would ever ask," says General John Michael Loh, commander of the Air Force's Air Combat Command.[2] Regardless of your role, being part of the military means agreeing to fight and, if necessary, even die for your country.

This dramatic difference in civilian and military expectations and lifestyle may leave those exiting the military at a loss as to how to proceed. They are not only leaving a job, but a total way of life. They not only have career issues to deal with, but also have to make decisions about housing, schooling, training, health insurance and social involvement, often all for the very first time.

At the same time, military people have been trained to be in control, and to know how to take control. So it's especially difficult when they must relinquish some control in the civilian work world. Add in the multitude of decisions that need to be made and the situation can seem overwhelming. "There's too much choice and it's frustrating," says a retired Air Force master sergeant. "My wife says I'm afraid of making a decision. But my whole senses are just being flooded—you don't know where you are going, what you're doing. We used to live in base housing. Everything was arranged—a house, jobs. So for me, it's a real mental strain."[3]

Staying in Control

If you are one of the many exiting the military, it's important not to let circumstances overtake your good judgment and render you frozen or ineffectual.

First of all, just allow yourself to acknowledge and accept the strains of your current predicament. Realizing that you are in a stressful situation that is going to be emotionally and mentally demanding can be a relief in itself. You need not spend time and energy worrying about why you feel the way you do if you know that the way you feel is normal.

One way to look at it is that how you feel may be similar to how visitors feel coming to a new country. Suddenly everything is different—the culture, the language, the economy and even the food. Entering civilian life can be similarly disorienting. Because many military families have frequently moved, they think of themselves as being adaptable and, perhaps, immune to the stress caused by this type of change. However, there's a difference now. Moves made within the military still result in your living in a military culture; while the states or countries may vary, the practices and norms of day-to-day life don't change that much. But even if you stay in the same city, the changes experienced in leaving the military and entering civilian life can be as dramatic as moving from New York City to the Sahara Desert.

Understanding the Inside-And-Outside Differences

Take an honest look at the fundamental differences between jobs in the military and jobs in the civilian world. A critical area is the contrast in *authority* and *responsibility*. Officers who carve successful career paths in the military are given a lot of authority and responsibility, often at an early age, which increases as their careers progress. For example, a newly promoted lieutenant's first assignment in his new rank was tank platoon commander. In this position, he was responsible for literally tens of millions of dollars worth of hardware and the very lives of 25 recruits. When this man ended his military career at age 42, he had risen to the rank of major and was overseeing supplies for 100,000 Army reservists, a job entailing the management of a $23 million operating budget as well as facilities spread out across half the nation.[4]

In the civilian world, a job with this much authority and responsibility would be a senior-management job, while in the military, it is more of a middle-management position. The average 42-year-old civilian in middle management would not have this much authority or responsibility. He or she is much more likely to be managing a staff of five to 30 and may not even have responsibility for an operating budget. If a budget is within his or her jurisdiction, it's more likely to be around $500,000 to several million, depending on the industry and size of the company.

When people like the 42-year-old major make the transition into the civilian work world, they are often in for a surprise. Military officers find themselves having to accept positions with far less authority and responsibility than they were accustomed to. The major, for example, eventually landed a job where he was part of a team, rather than the "undisputed leader of a small army of logistics experts."[5]

While this kind of change can be hard, it is *critical to realize that it may be necessary in order for you to make the transition.* You must develop and maintain a realistic *civilian-world* perspective. The major took his new civilian position and started it with the right attitude: "For some guys, [this kind of step down is] hard to take," he said, ". . . but getting in is what's important."[6]

Unfortunately, it's also likely that a decrease in authority and responsibility will be reflected in a decrease in pay. In fact, your salary may be lower just because the 1990-1991 recession caused a decrease in management salaries, while the earlier buildup of American defense pushed military pay up. A 43-year-old colonel with 22 years of service may earn $80,000, and even captains in the Army and Air Force in their early thirties or lieutenants in the Navy with 10 years of service can be earning $43,000. By contrast, the U.S. Bureau of Labor reported that the 1991 median annual salaries for managers ranged from $32,000 for those in public administration to $41,000 for those in purchasing, marketing and public relations.[7]

One thing that can help here is military retirement pay. An officer with 20 years of service can collect between $22,000 and $80,000 and have access to military health services, low-cost commissaries and other perks. Even younger military personnel are being offered yearly payments or single lump payments that can help cushion the financial transition from military to civilian life.[8]

Sizing Up the Civilian Situation

Understand that the impact of moving from the military to the civilian work world will be intensified by changes that have already occurred in the civilian workforce, most significantly the shrinking number of management positions in all industries.

The kinds of management jobs usually sought by military personnel have been severely cut back in the civilian workforce. This means that there are fewer positions and more competition than there would normally be.

This narrowing of opportunity has been just as big a shock for the management staff already in the civilian workforce. Many were themselves laid off. Others, while still employed, have found their opportunities severely curtailed. Civilian-side managers have been pushed into accepting the new workforce reality and looking at different kinds of opportunities or advancement emerging from it. Sometimes they have been forced to completely change their careers and leave management for another field.

Management-level ex-military individuals entering the civilian workforce need to make the same kinds of adjustments as those of civilian managers. This is hard, but true, and it pays to acknowledge reality early on so you can deal with it. "Military people have to realize that in today's job market they may not get a middle-management or upper-management job . . . sometimes they've got to start two or three rungs down the ladder," says Doug Carter, director of job placement for the Retired Officers Association (ROA) in Alexandria, Virginia. Military people ". . . may have to reorient their thinking completely, to accept a job as one of a team, to go into sales or become a teacher."[9] Now is when some of the decision-making and survival skills learned during military training can be put to use to take on the challenges of moving into the civilian work world. "I don't expect someone to hire me in top management right away. I'm willing to enter wherever I can get in," says a colonel who may have to retire. "I've always been a survivor and I'm pretty flexible."[10]

The defense industry has traditionally been a haven for those making a career transition from the military. While part of the corporate world, defense contractors share many of the same work values, cultures and practices of the military. Going to work for a defense company from the military has probably been the easiest, most comfortable move for ex-military personnel to make.

Unfortunately, the same cuts in defense spending that are downsizing the military are also shrinking the private sector of the defense industry. As a result, this traditional market for employment has drastically diminished. In the 1980s, defense-contractor jobs accounted for 40 percent of the positions listed with a national job bank maintained by the Reserve Officers Association. In 1992, that figure was down to 25 percent.[11]

Selling Your Strengths

Realize that you are starting a new career and that this is not an overnight achievement. If you are like the typical person exiting the military, you may not have fully absorbed this concept until you actually left your job. "The average military person [will] work until the last day and come in here and ask me, 'What's the next step?'" says ROA's Carter.[12]

The "next step" is a lot of hard work and effort. First of all, you are an unknown entity in the commercial world. You need to take the responsibility for showing how your skills and experience will translate into a civilian job. The commercial world does not have a clear picture of what people in the military do. They may want to hire you, but they don't understand how your experience applies to their business. "The perception of military officers in the U.S. commercial and private sector is that what these people have done doesn't count, because they haven't dealt in pre-packaged widgets—that what they have done isn't profit-oriented, manufacturing-oriented, product-oriented," claims Bob McCarthy, president of McCarthy Resource Associates, a California management placement firm.[13] It's your responsibility to show them that it does count by showing the parallels between your experience in a generic sense and what commercial employers are looking for.

Familiarize yourself with the business world. You need to learn about potential career-move occupations, how to access your military experience and how to "translate" it into non-military terms. Do this by taking advantage of career services being offered to the military through government-funded or private programs and agencies. Federal and state dollars have been allocated to assist ex-military personnel with career planning. State and local employee agencies may have special programs to assist you. There are also privately funded groups, such as the Retired Officers Association, offering assistance.

Learn the basic career exploration and job search skills. (See Chapter 17, Job Search, as well as the Afterword and Suggested Reading sections.) Include a visit to the library or bookstore as one of your first steps. Check out job support groups, networking and career counselors. A small investment in some expert advice could pay off with a more focused, knowledgeable and, therefore, shorter job search.

Look at the task of redirecting your career as you would any challenge: Become as knowledgeable as you can, know your strengths, cope with your weaknesses and, above all, have the courage and determination to move forward. It is the only direction to go.

 MINORITIES

I n the next 15 years, two-thirds of the nation's new workers will be minorities.[1] By the year 2005, minorities will
compose 27 percent of the workforce, up from 22 percent in
1993.[2] Together, minorities and women will account for approximately 62 percent of the workforce in 2005, making white
males a minority for the first time.[3]

Cultural Diversity

As a result of this shift, "cultural diversity" is emerging as
a critical issue in the workplace. Cultural diversity addresses
the positive recognition of employees' cultural and ethnic differences and the need to manage them accordingly. Virtually
all companies, from the most conservative to the most progressive, must recognize and deal with these differences, not
only to meet government-mandated requirements, but to improve workforce morale and productivity.

Founded on predominately "white-male" work ethics and
practices, companies are often unaware of or, worse, intoler-
ant of cultural differences. In turn, minority employees often
don't realize that their perspective may be different from that
of their employers or, if they do, may not understand the true
impact of this difference. For example, a Hispanic manager,
often coming from a culture where decision-making is a group
process with much discussion and consultation, can encoun-

ter problems when he or she assumes a role that requires independent and individual decision making.

The result of "cultural insensitivity" can be confusion, miscommunication and a loss of opportunity for both companies and workers, as individual needs are not addressed and/or individual talents go unrecognized. A number of Asian-Americans, for example, imbued with traditional Asian modesty and reserve, are uncomfortable or unfamiliar with the need to "blow their own horn" to get ahead in the average American organization. This can make them "invisible" and prevent their employers from using their undiscovered skills and talents.

In a study of 94 large U.S. companies, 15.5 percent of the employees were minorities, but they accounted for only 6 percent of total management and 2.6 percent of upper management.[4] In fact, the number of minorities in upper management in American companies has remained virtually unchanged since 1979, having risen from 3 percent to 5 percent, a statistically insignificant increase.[5] This same scarcity also exists at the board-of-director level. Today, among 801 of the Fortune 1000 companies, African-Americans and Hispanics account for only 3 percent of the directorships held, the same as in 1987, while few, if any, Asian-Americans hold seats.[6]

Big Company Programs

To cope with the changing workforce, companies are forming *cultural diversity programs*. Their purposes are multifold, focusing on not only recruiting minorities, but also on mentoring and promoting minority employees from within. This is crucial because while many companies have internal employee-development programs, minorities are often "overlooked," and/or minority employees may not even be aware of such programs. In addition to dealing with recruitment and promotion, good cultural-diversity programs are training both managers and employees to recognize, understand and work with cultural differences in the workplace.

In 1990, a diversity task force with members from a cross section of ethnic groups from industry, education and community backgrounds was formed by Pacific Bell to offer suggestions for improving the company's employee practices and community involvement programs. The task force also sought to assure that women-owned businesses, minority and disabled entrepreneurs achieve maximum participation in the award of contracts. Results were enthusiastically received by the utilities industry which is using the task force's findings as a model for the development of its own programs.[7]

The cultural-diversity program at Lotus Development retrains managers to "see beyond" color and gender and recognize how an individual's skills can meet company needs, irrespective of a person's ethnicity. Most cultural-diversity programs also focus on ensuring that this "rethinking" is extended to recognizing and promoting talented minority individuals. Recognizing talent in someone who may be different from you is a key issue in cultural-diversity programs, since, for many in management, ethnic differences can cloud the recognition of true talent. While people want to hire or promote the best candidate, "the problem is that most people think 'best' means just like me," says Stuart Kazin, vice president for manufacturing and distribution at Lotus.[8]

To get minorities onto the "career tracks" in a company, well-planned cultural-diversity programs need to encompass all levels of an organization, so that all minority employees are shown that getting on a *career path* means more than just "doing a job" both at the beginning and throughout their careers.

Minorities often don't hire on in "key, career-oriented" positions or receive the initial job promotions necessary to get on the road to management. As a result, they don't have the training and experience to move into middle- and upper-management positions. "We now know that we need to put together a guide to what are the key jobs someone should hold to be among the next generation of senior financial executives," says Margie Filter, corporate treasurer for Xerox, commenting on the company's efforts to close this career-strategy information gap.[9]

Companies are creating different ways to develop career-track programs for minorities. S.C. Johnson & Son (formerly Johnson's Wax) has developed a plan to identify "high potential employees and match each with an executive sponsor" who helps the employee map out a 10-year career plan.[10] At Levi Strauss & Co., part of management bonuses is tied to demonstrably "appreciating" diversity by meeting the goals of the company's cultural diversity "Aspiration Statement."[11] At Lotus, a cross-training program allows employees to work in another part of the company for one day every week for six months to expand their knowledge and experience. A mentoring program also exists where middle-management volunteers take on a "protégé" from another department. Protégés and mentors meet for four hours a month for 12 months, discussing everything from company structure and job opportunities to appropriate dress and work style.[12]

Small Companies on the Bandwagon

Cultural-diversity programs developed by large companies tend to receive the most public attention. Already highly visible, organizations like Xerox, Gannet, Corning, Merck and Monsanto, because of their size, have more cultural issues to deal with, more resources to devote to them, and garner more public recognition for their efforts than smaller organizations. But small companies are also working on the issues. A study of 79 small companies with annual sales of less than $50 million showed that 58 percent of the companies cited a need for change in cultural attitudes, 54 percent wanted to improve employee communication, 49 percent saw the need for more training, and 37 percent felt they must develop more job opportunities. Fifty-five percent had already developed programs to improve communications, and more than half were offering various kinds of training. In an effort to recognize cultural differences, 38 percent were giving minority employees time to observe religious holidays, and 15 percent were restructuring their benefit plans with options attractive to minorities.[13]

Outside Organizations

Cultural-diversity training is also available outside corporations. In the private sector, training specialists and providers offer courses and seminars. Groups like the American Management Association offer courses and conferences. Colleges and universities have already begun changing their curriculum to include cultural-diversity and gender issues. At the University of California at Irvine (UCI) Extension Program, all continuing-education students, usually working adults, who are enrolled in the school's 41 certificate programs are required to take at least one three-hour course in cultural diversity. UCI's program is the first in the country to offer multicultural training to working individuals (other than teachers of non-English-speaking students or managers and human relations staff involved with state and federal anti-discrimination regulations). "No matter what field you are in today, whether it's emergency response, health care or engineering, anyone who is in a professional field involving other people—either directly or indirectly—needs to have some appreciation for the impacts of culture," says Melvin E. Hall, UCI's dean of extended education programs.

Following the UCI lead, the National University Continuing Education Association has developed a task force to bring diversity and gender issues into the forefront of continuing-education programs.[14]

Tackling the Issues

Ultimately, the success of cultural-diversity training, regardless of where it is offered, depends on changes in thinking. Both whites and minorities need to address and dispel the belief systems that perpetuate discrimination. There is a long-standing myth that African-Americans "lack motivation." Yet, throughout most of the 20th century, African-Americans have been more likely to work than whites. There was a greater percentage of African-American men in the workforce from 1890 until after World War II, and a higher rate of African-American women held jobs than did white women until the mid-1990s. Today, after a 25-year influx of white women in the workplace, white and African-American women are in the workforce in virtually even numbers. And even with the difficulties of the current job market and environment, 69.5 percent of African-American men are employed, a rate only slightly less than the 76.4 percent for white men.[15]

Hispanics compose another group often maligned in terms of its work ethic. In Los Angeles, where one out of every four people is Hispanic, fewer Hispanics are on public assistance programs than any other racial group, including whites. Ninety-four percent of Hispanic homes have at least one member employed full time and typically everyone over 18 is employed.[16]

In addition to defeating cultural myths, there are problematic issues to be solved. Hispanics are highly underrepresented in professional and corporate occupations because they often are undereducated, which keeps them out of the mainstream of corporate America, despite their strong work ethic. Similarly, while African-Americans are three times more likely to graduate from college today than 20 years ago, they are still undereducated as a group, frequently barring them from much of the workplace.[17]

Of those attending college, both African-Americans and Hispanics are less likely to major in science or engineering than Asian-American students and traditionally have been discouraged from pursuing these careers. In 1988, only three African-Americans graduated with degrees in the physical sciences from the entire University of California system.[18] Many talented minorities are dissuaded from these career choices. When he expressed his career goals to his high school counselor, Celestino Beltran, now president and CEO of a $33.4 million software-development company, was told, "Mexicans don't make good engineers," and the counselor recommended he learn mechanics instead.[19]

Asian-Americans often have a different problem. As a group, they have gained recognition in the workplace for their technical competence but are overlooked when it comes to management. At Hughes Aircraft, for example, Asian-Americans comprise 24 percent of the technical staff, but account for only 5 percent of managers. Similar disparities exist at TRW where they make up 20 percent of aerospace, engineering and science employees, but only 11 percent of management.[20] Often their exclusion from management has been complicated by security regulations, which may automatically exempt foreign-born employees from key positions.

The non-promotion of minorities can only stunt the growth of business by hindering the effective use of its most important asset—people. In California, for example, it is estimated that half of all new aerospace engineers will be Asian-Americans.[21] If they can't be promoted into management, important leadership will be lost and the industry itself will suffer. "If you don't have an environment that can embrace all comers, then you deprive yourself of much of the talent in society," says Reid Ashe, publisher of the *Wichita Eagle.*[22]

What to Do

To deny that it can be more difficult to get ahead if you come from a minority is to deny reality. Racial minorities, like other special groups, such as older workers, women and the disabled, often must strive harder to advance, and face greater setbacks.

Attitude counts heavily in your chances for success. It is easy to fall into the "minority syndrome"—assuming you aren't hired or promoted simply because you are a minority. Companies hire and promote qualified candidates and seek out those who have taken the time to understand their needs, policies and philosophy. They are looking to bring in and advance people who will put out the extra effort to investigate position requirements, train to fill them, and do their best to support the employer by understanding his or her company problems and challenges and working to solve them. If you meet these criteria and are passed over, your minority status may be an issue. If you don't, you must make that essential effort to become the most desirable candidate. In addition to presenting your qualifications persuasively in your résumé and interviews, you must have a positive attitude, persistence and determination. These are critical to your success, as is getting as much education and training as possible.

Education and Training

Evaluate your education. Minorities often enter the workforce with less education than others, so it may be necessary to take courses or pursue a first or even second degree. If you decide additional schooling is necessary, thoroughly explore training offered within your company. If you need to take outside classes or get a degree or certificate, find out if educational assistance programs are available from your employer. If they aren't, ask anyway. Even if they can't offer monetary assistance, often companies will work with individuals to help them "go back to school" by altering work schedules, shifting workloads or making other accommodations.

Tapping Cultural-Diversity Opportunities

While an awareness of demographic changes and cultural-diversity programs may not solve your career problems overnight, it may help you use the workplace to your advantage. Find out if any special programs exist in your company. If they don't, see if you can get something started.

Speak up for yourself, point out your accomplishments, ask for raises and promotions. Don't take advancement for granted and then quietly fume if it doesn't happen. You must ask. If there are attitude or style differences between you and your employer, try to recognize them and determine what you both can do to work them out. Like any other employee, you must gain an understanding of the culture of the organization you work for. If you accept this culture, then you must make an effort to fit into it. This does not mean sacrificing your individuality or tolerating prejudice, but it does mean having the same responsibility as others to try to work effectively with your organization, rather than against it.

Ultimately, differences between individuals and organizations are worked out through a combination of attempting to understand, granting respect, accepting some things about the other and being willing to change certain things about themselves. "My way" and "your way" have to be combined into "our way," with both the employer and the employee taking responsibility to make it happen.

Entrepreneurship

If you have special skills or talents and the financial resources to take the risk, you may want to consider starting your own business. (See Chapter 9, Going On Your Own.) Some minority groups, like Hispanics, have historically been community leaders in entrepreneurial efforts. Entrepreneurship is an increasingly attractive alternative to the mainstream American workplace, as many women and older workers are finding. Between 1982 and 1987, African-American business ownership rose 38 percent; Hispanic ownership was up 81 percent; Native American, 58 percent; and Asian-Americans showed the largest increase at 89 percent. This trend is expected to continue.[23]

Taking a Positive Attitude

Regardless of what path you choose, you must develop and maintain a positive attitude. "By definition, you're not in the majority. You can't worry about it though," says J. Bruce Llewellyn, CEO of Philadelphia Cola-Cola Bottling, the third-largest black-owned company in the nation. "You have to ask: 'What can I do for myself?' . . . Then go out and do it. A positive attitude is critical. This is a prejudiced society. It's not going to go away. But you can still succeed."[24]

15.

OLDER WORKERS

Redefining Retirement

"Retirement" used to have a clear-cut definition. We worked, we saved, and then we stopped working—we retired. Retirement might occur because we reached a specific age mandated by our employers as to when we had to quit. Or we reached a point where, economically, we did not have to work any longer, but could rely on some combination of savings, pensions and Social Security.

Like most things in today's workplace, why and how we go about retiring has also changed. First, retirement often isn't voluntary anymore. In the past, most people not only looked forward to retiring, they also assumed they would be able to choose *when* they would retire. Sure, there were always high-energy workers who didn't want to put the brakes on at 65 or 70. And many of them retired unhappily and found their new lifestyle adversely affected their happiness, health and even, it is sometimes argued, their lifespan. But they were considered to be a minority, whether or not they actually were.

One of the most common ways companies are downsizing in the 1990s is by offering, or sometimes forcing, early retirement on employees who are not ready for it. In a study conducted by the Wyatt Co., a management consulting firm, 14 of 50 large companies reported they began offering early-retirement incentives in 1991.[1] Between 1991 and 1992, for example, Hewlett Packard, Ameritech, Southwestern Bell, Bell Atlantic, Philip Morris, Houston Lighting & Power, Western Resources and Transco Energy all initiated early-retirement programs.[2] As part of efforts to voluntarily reduce its workforce, IBM instituted more than 87 separate early-retirement and buy-out programs as incentives.[3] Even the military has begun offering unprecedented early-retirement programs to younger officers who, because of their shorter length of service, previously would not have been eligible for any retirement pay.

As a result, people are retiring at ages much younger than what we traditionally think of as appropriate retirement age. **Early retirement is often not welcome.** In a 1991 Gallup Poll of baby boomers (those born between 1946 and 1964), 66 percent wanted to retire somewhere between the ages of 61 and 70+. Seven percent said they never wanted to retire. Only 25 percent wanted to retire at age 50 or under, and only 19 percent between the age of 56 and 60.[4] A 1992 survey conducted for *U.S. News & World Report* showed that 45 percent of the 1,200 adults surveyed currently worked or expected to work after the age of 65.

For many, early retirement is hitting much sooner than financial stability. Today, Americans in their fifties and even sixties are often paying mortgages and putting children through college. Sometimes, they have started to contribute to the support of their own parents. Often described as the "sandwich generation," they may even have to support grown children forced to move back "home" as a result of their own financial misfortunes.

At the same time, the current group of early retirees is likely to have less money saved than those in the past. The savings rate for Americans was 4 percent in 1991, down from an average of 7 percent in the 1960s and a peak of 9.4 percent in 1974. In fact, the baby boomers are beginning midlife with the lowest rate of personal savings recorded.[5]

Longer lifespans are often necessitating longer careers. Since the beginning of the century, life expectancy has increased to an average of 75 years. Because we are living longer, most of us will need to work longer, as much as 50 years of our 75-year lifespan.

And some people, regardless of their age, don't want to stop working even if they can financially afford to. For these people, retirement at an "appropriate" age is not welcome, and early retirement is an anathema. For some, the "golden years" of retirement are not considered a cherished goal. People identify strongly with their work—it is part of who they are. This identity doesn't cease to be important just because a certain birthday rolls along. For many, golf, grandchildren and gardening just won't do it. Maggie Kuhn, founder of the Gray Panthers, said, "People should have a lifelong opportunity to work. . . . Personally I want to die in an airport, briefcase in hand, mission accomplished."[6]

Changing Your Attitudes

Older unemployed people who still wish or need to work must take several steps. They must understand the work environment, acknowledge and cope with their own feelings, and carefully analyze the pros and cons of their situation. Then they can take the most important step—*they must let go of the past and think in terms of "next."* This means abandoning the idea of one career and the notion that one shouldn't have to start over. It means accepting the concept of second and third careers and, correspondingly, of first, second and even third "retirements." Our work life, it turns out, may be cyclical and repetitive, rather than having a defined beginning, middle and end. In a practical sense, this attitude revision will help develop a strategy to get back into the workforce when you want to and, preferably, on terms that you choose.

Getting It Together

If you are unexpectedly retired, or facing retirement, and still want and/or need to work, take the time to absorb the reality of your situation and allow yourself to experience your feelings. The situation is a painful one which, like other painful things in life, may include trauma, a sense of loss or simply rough going. You may feel a combination of anger, confusion, fear and sadness. All this emotion shouldn't bring you to a dead stop, causing you to wallow in your misery, refusing to move on. Rather, you should let yourself be human and give yourself the same break, the same care and comfort you would a friend in a similar situation. And as you would expect your friend to carry on, so must you.

It is critical that you make plans and work to get re-employed. It's okay if you don't know exactly how to proceed or precisely what you will do. Take the steps to find out how to proceed. *You must not give up.* You don't want to emulate some of New Jersey employment attorney Nancy Erika's older clients, who she says, "gain a hundred pounds and start drinking heavily" in response to a job loss.[7]

Expect to feel unsettled. Carol Humple Seagrave, a consultant for older workers with TTG Consultants in California, calls this condition the "neutral zone," a difficult stage between the initial jolt of joblessness and the start of something new.[8] It's natural to find yourself in the neutral zone. Just don't let yourself stay there.

Tackling Age Discrimination

Unfortunately, age discrimination is alive and well, although in theory age is not supposed to matter. Laws have been passed and new ones will follow them to prevent it. In 1967, the Age Discrimination Employment Act was enacted to "protect workers over 40 from bias in hiring, wages and fringe benefits." In 1990, this original litigation was amended with the enactment of the Older Workers Benefit Protection Act.[9]

Despite legislative pressure and corporate statements of goodwill and intentions, an increasing number of older workers have continued to experience discrimination since the

1990-1991 recession. Many feel that the recession is affecting older workers disproportionately. In 1991, the American Association of Retired Persons (AARP) received 105,000 requests for information on age discrimination, a 155-percent increase from the previous year. During that same year, the Equal Employment Opportunity Commission (EEOC) reported that age-discrimination cases jumped 20 percent to a total of 17,449 after having dropped in the four previous years prior to the recession.[10]

The Ins and Outs and Shoves of Early Retirement

Age discrimination is even harder to prove when early retirement offers are *accepted* by employees, which is most often the case. Of the 14 companies who told Wyatt Consultants they had initiated early retirement programs, 10 said the number of employee acceptances had "met corporate goals."[11]

What actually goes on behind the acceptance of every early retirement plan can only be guessed at. Obviously, it depends on the individual and the company. It seems probable, however, by looking at the number of EEOC claims filed and the number of information requests received by AARP, that not everyone is *going willingly*, and that some feel a degree of coercion or sense of being *forced out*. Technically, acceptance of early retirement is voluntary, says New York attorney David A. Field, "[but] responsibilities might be taken away, you might be assigned to a smaller office, and after years of good job appraisals you might start getting bad ones." Things like these are called "getting rough treatment" by the experts. Cathy Ventrell-Monsees, an AARP attorney, says, "The easiest barometer is to compare your treatment with the treatment of someone else in a job like yours. Are you getting assignments similar to others? Are you included in the same kinds of meetings? Are you offered similar training opportunities?"[12]

Prejudices and Stereotypes

American culture, with its perennial emphasis on youth, is accustomed to looking less favorably on those who are older, both in and out of the workplace. Ken Dychtwald and Joe Flower, the authors of *Age Wave*, say, "Our culture is deeply gerontophobic. We have a fear of aging and a prejudice against the old that clouds all our perceptions about what it means to grow old in America."[13]

On the bright side, however, the number of older Americans is increasing in the United States and easing the stigma of being older, just as workplace changes increased the number of jobless and lessened the stigma of "unemployment." With over 13 percent of the population age 65 or older by the year 2000, the number of older people in this country will reach "critical mass and set the course for American society," says Dychtwald.[14]

In the past, many felt older workers would not be effective in the workforce because they lacked the necessary qualities, attitudes and abilities. Myths and stereotypes about older workers have abounded as part of our "old-age" phobia, including misconceptions that they are incapacitated by chronic health problems, beset by memory loss and learning disabilities, less energetic, slower and less creative than younger workers or, worse, resistant to change, stubborn and unable to get along with others.

Although false, these stereotypes continue to be perpetuated in the workforce. While older workers may have chronic health problems, they are usually controlled and do not necessarily affect their work patterns. In fact, **older workers have better attendance than younger workers**. They also stay on the job longer. According to AARP, workers in their fifties and sixties will stay on the job an average of 15 years, as opposed to employees in their twenties and thirties who typically change positions every 3.4 years. The Bureau of Labor says workers aged 45 to 65 have lower turnover rates than workers who are 45 or younger.[15]

Days Inns of America and Travelers Corporation are two companies that actively recruit older workers because they want to avoid the absenteeism and high turnover of younger employees. Days Inns found that its over-50 employees learned its computerized reservation systems as quickly as younger workers and booked more reservations than younger employees. And because older workers stayed three times longer than younger ones, Days Inns found its hiring costs dropping to $600 per employee from $1700, as a result of lower employee turnover.[16]

The majority of older workers do not have problems with their memory. A study in the late 1980s showed only 10 percent of the more than 30 million Americans over age 65 were estimated to have a significant loss of memory. And older workers ranked as well or better than their younger colleagues in creativity, decisiveness and judgment skills. They differed only in the ways in which they processed information, not the ability to do so. Even with small declines in short-term memorization ability and mental quickness, older workers were able to analyze information and situations better and make better judgments (and fewer errors) than younger workers. Some experts say they have greater "chunking" skills—the ability to organize information in useful and logical ways, which is necessary in finding solutions to complex, real-world problems.[17]

Overall, older workers are a great labor resource. The Department of Labor, the Senate Committee on Human Resources and studies in gerontology publications such as the *Journal of Gerontology* and *Industrial Gerontology* have shown that, in all areas, from semiskilled to sales people and executives, older workers were shown to perform as well or better than their younger counterparts, except for a slight decline in productivity in jobs requiring substantial physical effort. But even in areas of physical effort, the older worker's better judgment plays a key factor. In the early 1980s, while seniors made up 13.6 percent of the labor force, they accounted for only 9.7 percent of worker-related accidents, while workers between the ages of 20 and 24 accounted for 50 percent of total worker-related accidents. Also, sheer physical effort is becoming less important since the basis for many jobs is shifting to knowledge, judgment and experience.[18]

Taking on the Real World

Older workers looking for work, however, often find that their positive attributes are not common knowledge. In reality, they frequently experience a rougher time getting hired and face more obstacles than younger job seekers. Therefore, they have to work harder to find new positions. Older workers need to be persuasive, determined and persistent. As one 60-year-old who hasn't had to look for a job since he was 35 says, "I feel I have to go that extra effort to stand out above everyone else."[19]

Here are a few tactics for tackling today's job market:

1. **Be prepared to put a lot of time and effort into your job search. You may be lucky and find something quickly, but statistics show it is taking older workers more time to find positions than younger ones.** Charles Grisdale, a partner with Aim Executive Consulting in Troy, Michigan, found laid-off workers 55 to 65 years old take an average of three months longer to find work than younger workers, a fact backed by an Exec-U-Net poll of its job-seeking executive membership.[20]

2. **Present yourself persuasively.** While you don't want to emphasize the age issue, don't ignore it either. Instead, turn it into a positive by pointing out the benefits of your experience and skills. William K. Ellermeyer, a senior vice president with outplacement firm Lee Hecht Harrison in Irvine, California, says, "I don't think age is as much of a factor as it was in the '70s. The key words are 'quality' and 'productivity.' Companies are more willing to hire someone who is 54 because you get an early return on your investment." You must show you are adaptable, can cope with change, and have the needed stamina and determination. "The key thing is energy," Ellermeyer adds. "You can find an energetic person who is 62 and someone at 40 who acts like it's all over."[21]

3. **Look into starting your own business.** Like job seekers of any age, opening a business, if it interests you and you feel you have marketable talents and skills, may be a good alternative. Between 1981 and 1991, the number of self-employed workers age 55 and older rose 11 percent to almost two million.[22] This growth is expected to continue. In 1992, 87.5 percent of laid-off managers who opted for self-employment were 40 or older, up from 63.5 percent in 1991.[23] (See chapters in Part Three: Paving New Ground.)

4. **Look into smaller companies.** Lean by nature, small companies are looking for people who can wear several different hats, and who can analyze, conceptualize, come to and implement good decisions in their multiple roles. Older workers, with their extensive and often multifaceted backgrounds, are frequently filling key positions in these companies.

5. **Look at temporary and part-time opportunities.** Some companies, suffering from the deficit of talent they have created as a result of cutbacks, are hiring experienced people (often their own former employees) on a part-time or consulting basis to get back the expertise they need.

Travelers Corporation has an in-house temporary service it staffs mostly with its own retirees. Travelers estimates it has saved about $900,000 a year because retirees already know the company and can be instantly productive even in temporary situations.[24]

Some temporary-service companies have special programs for older workers. Kelly Services, for example, has a program called Encore: The Kelly Services Program for Mature Workers. Through Encore, Kelly provides free training to temporary workers 55 and older.[25]

6. **Research what kinds of careers and industries are being touted as especially good for older workers.** There are many excellent sources profiling opportunities. *Second Careers: New Ways to Work After 50*, by Caroline Bird (Little Brown, 1992), is a book based on research from the American Association of Retired Persons' *Modern Maturity* maga-

zine.[26] There are also government and private agencies and organizations that specialize in assisting older workers with career direction. Find out what is available to you through your local library or employment office.

Be Your Own Advocate

Above all, be diligent and don't give up. Older job seekers are sometimes their own worst enemy because they internally accept the negative stereotypes and become depressed and defeated. Instead, you have to convince prospective employers and yourself that ". . . you have a fresh view of things and that your experience will help you find the answers—not make you inflexible," says a 52-year-old re-employed engineer. You must look at the age issue as a challenge, and not be done in by it. He adds, "You should remember how good you are, how much you know."[27] And convince someone else of this. One person, that's all it takes.

16.  WOMEN

Women in the Workplace

Women and work has always been a heated issue. Since the beginning of the century, we have seen a never-ending cycle of controversy, debate, resolution and stalemate, regularly refueled as new women-in-the-workplace issues erupt, old ones re-emerge and many just simmer along, continually demanding attention and effort.

While things have definitely changed, women have not "caught up" with men in the work world in terms of pay, opportunity, status or recognition. They still hold lower-ranking jobs and make less money. Even the few that do get into the upper echelons of management average less money than their male counterparts. And there are entire fields and occupations where women have virtually no presence.

The "gap" between what men and women make in equivalent jobs has shrunk, in part, because men's salaries are declining. Since men generally make more money and hold more higher-level positions, they have been more greatly impacted by white-collar wage reductions and layoffs, which came with the 1990-1991 recession, and have now been forced to take lower-paying new jobs. "When you look at the figures for women in the median-pay bracket, the narrowing of the gap in the '80s was about 75 percent due to men's wages falling, not female wage growth," says Jared Bernstein of The Economic Policy Institute.[1] In 1977, women earned 59 cents for every dollar earned by men, and by 1991, they earned 74 cents for every "male" dollar.[2]

Besides being plagued by lower pay, women's careers generally progress more slowly and not as far as those of men. While women account for almost half of the workforce in the United States, they hold less than 5 percent of the top management positions in America's largest organizations. True, low- and middle-management positions held by women have risen from 27 percent in 1981 to 41 percent in 1991.[3] But as former Labor Secretary Lynn Martin states, "We continue to find a general absence of . . . women at the highest levels in the corporate work force, in the developmental programs and in the credential-building assignments."[4] This scarcity of women at senior levels is seen as well in the makeup of boards of directors in America's corporations where only 7.5 percent of the slots are held by women.[5]

A look into many industries shows women trail in the perceived value of their experience and education, the status of their rank and the amount of their pay. Women make up less than 15 percent of large law firm partners and federal and state judgeships.[6] In 1992, women doctors earned median incomes that were 27.8 percent less than male colleagues.[7] Fifty-five percent of all women holding state and local government jobs are "stuck" in jobs whose salaries averaged *below* $20,000.[8] In 1993, while women accounted for two-out-of-three new members and 40 percent of all unions' membership, their management participation was only 20 percent in local unions, 8 percent on national boards, and only two of the country's 86 AFL-CIO presidents were women.[9] Across the board, women still lack a critical presence.

The Glass Ceiling

The term, "glass ceiling," was originally coined in the 1987 book, *Breaking the Glass Ceiling*,[10] and it is truly a great metaphor. The term refers to an invisible barrier preventing entrance to the top jobs. Its imagery works well because, like a clear sheet of glass, not everybody can see it; thus, there's a lot of argument over whether or not it really exists. Some people claim to be seriously wounded from bumping into it, while others are sure there is no such thing and seem unable to see or touch it. The perception of the glass ceiling in the workplace varies from person to person and company to company.

A 1991 U.S. Department of Labor two-year blind study of nine Fortune 500 companies found that all had a level beyond which few women were recruited. Or to put it plainly, the glass ceiling existed at a much lower level than first thought.[11] In a survey conducted by *BusinessWeek*, half of the 400 female managers surveyed felt that Corporate America was doing "somewhat better" in terms of hiring and promoting women, while the other half felt that progress has slowed.[12]

The Brighter Side

While many may dispute the amount of progress women are making in the workplace, there is a general consensus that progress is being made and, perhaps more importantly, that demographic and workplace trends and circumstances are in place to support and further that progress. In *Megatrends for Women*, authors Patricia Aburdene and John Naisbitt say that women will move into equal status in every aspect of life because the women's movement has reached "critical mass."[13]

The number of women in the workplace has certainly hit critical mass. While women may account for less than 5 percent of senior management, they do make up 46 percent of the workforce and hold 41 percent of management positions. By the year 2000, there will be an entire generation of women in the workforce who have been full-time careerists and who have amassed 20 to 30 years of experience. This group is creating the first "labor pool" from which experienced and qualified women can be recruited into higher-ranking positions. In most major corporations, 50 percent of the next group of managers below the top people are women.

The critical mass of women in the workplace is expected to help women move beyond "staff" jobs and into "line" areas and positions that have previously been male-dominated, like finance, marketing and manufacturing that really "run" a company, and from which senior management is frequently groomed and recruited. "Companies will want to mobilize the best talent. So there will be intense competition to recruit, develop and retain these women," says Felice N. Schwartz, president of Catalyst, Inc., a New York research firm specializing in women-at-work issues. If women don't quickly move into upper management ranks, says Anne Ronce, a San Francisco management consultant, "the amount of active discrimination would be so obvious as to be outrageous."[14]

Changes in Management Style

The trend in management is a shift from "bossing" to "facilitating." Rather than using a dictatorial, hands-off or reward/punishment approach, today's managers are having to lead by motivating, inspiring and eliciting cooperation and enthusiasm. This requirement has intensified as leaner-operating companies give their people more power and employees tend to work in teams. Managers realize they need to "empower" employees by sharing information and giving them the authority to make decisions and manage their own work, and that they and their teams must communicate across rank and function.

This is all good news for women who, according to some studies and researchers, may have already adopted this management style. "Women want to be powerful in ways that simultaneously enhance, rather than diminish, the power of others," says psychiatrist Jean Baker Miller, M.D., director of education for the Stone Center for Development Services and Studies at Wellesley College.[15]

Judy Rosener, a professor at the Graduate School of Management at the University of California at Irvine, defined women's management style in a 1990 landmark article in *The Harvard Business Journal*. Women, Rosener states, want to transform people's self-interest into organizational goals. She points to four major components in the way women manage that allow them to do this. Women "encourage participation, share power and information, enhance other people's self-worth and get others excited about their work."[16]

A study by the International Women's Forum showed that increased participation of women—as they rise in rank, manage and change the tenor and style of corporate culture—may be a key survival and success factor for America's companies.[17]

At the same time, it is important for women to recognize the difference between *behaving like a manager* versus *being a good girl*. While today's managers need to adopt a humanistic approach, they still need to *manage* in the true sense of the word. This means assuming a role of leadership, making sure things get done and reaching goals despite personnel issues. This doesn't mean they have to be abrasive, rude, or pushy (or the *verboten* "B" word). Women are often at an inherent disadvantage in this role because they have been taught to be "good," to keep everyone happy and not make waves. But good-girl behaviors will not lead to successful management. "The female executives who've climbed the corporate ladder are nontraditional," says Ann M. Morrison at the Center for Creative Leadership. "They've done things differently."[18]

Women also need to understand that the style and characteristics that got them into a management position need to be augmented by new behaviors in order for them to be effective managers and to continue to move up. "Once you reach middle management," says organization development consultant Neil Yeager, "the very thing that got you there—completing tasks, being acquiescent, working well with others—will keep you there and prevent you from getting to top-level positions if you don't *also* add some other important behaviors to your workplace repertoire." You have to be assertive, a strong leader, independent thinker and initiator, adds Yeager, not a dutiful employee.[19]

Women and Their Families and Work

No one has yet figured out how women can comfortably have and parent children and develop smooth careers at the same time. There are some "super women" who seem to do it all. Some manage but are exhausted and mortgage their personal lives for work and family. Others are assisted by nannies and worry if they spend enough time with their kids. Most wonder what's fair for themselves, their husbands and their children and constantly try to balance the equations.

Those who leave work for parenting often find their careers adversely affected, with their backs against "the maternal wall."[20] In a 1992 study, economists Joyce P. Jacobson and Laurence M. Levin compared the earnings of two groups of women with the same number of years of work experience in their field. The groups were the "gappers," women who had taken an average of three years off from their careers to raise children, and the "non-gappers," those who worked continually during their child-bearing years. One year after "gappers" returned to work, they were making 20 percent less than "non-gappers." And the discrepancy did not disappear. After 20 years, the "gappers" were still making 5 to 7 percent less.

Women who have "family timeouts" in their careers are looked upon differently than women who do not. Even after many years have gone by, employers may perceive them as less dedicated than those who kept on working say Jacobson and Levin, "This view may be reflected in reduced promotion possibilities, different job assignments and other actions that reduce wages."[21] "A woman who takes two years off to care for a baby is viewed as uncommitted to her career," says Marilyn Vito, CFO of Meridian Mortgage Corp. in Pennsylvania and president of the American Society of Women Accountants (ASWA). "But a man who does the same is 'progressive.'

I've heard a woman recruiter describe a man who took a two-year sabbatical to sail the East Coast as a dynamic personality who'd be an asset to any firm."[22]

Every woman must make her own decision, balancing time between work and family. It's a tough call and a personal one. Deborah Swiss and Judith Walker, authors of *Women and the Work/Family Dilemma*, were surprised to find that 25 percent of the female Harvard MBAs included in their study had left the workforce.[23]

However you choose to resolve the work/family dilemma, the important matter is to be aware of the issues you may face, and deal with them as they arise so that you can maintain as much control as possible over the pace of your career.

On the plus side, in today's workforce, qualified women may have the advantage, irrespective of their family situations. Since there is a projected labor shortage resulting from an inadequately educated workforce, women with strong educational backgrounds are expected to be an important resource that helps fill this gap. This could work particularly well for educated women "re-entering" the workforce from full-time parenting. In the past, these women may have been ignored; now the value of their education and experience will be recognized.

Women Out of Work

Women find it just as traumatic as men to lose their jobs. The sense of displacement, loss of identity, fear and anger are the same for women as they are for men. And with the large number of households dependent on two incomes and single parent households headed by women, the financial loss is often equally devastating.

Where men and women differ is in how they react to being unemployed. Men usually experience a lowering of self-esteem from the loss of income and status. Women experience this too; they also are more likely to blame themselves for having lost their jobs. This is a bad trap to fall into because blaming yourself just makes it harder to function in an already difficult situation.

Try to stay as objective as possible. If you are one of many who has been laid off, keep this in mind: *It's not personal. It was a company business decision.* You must hold this thought even if you were laid off while others were spared. You must realize that circumstances were out of your control; it's over and done, and you must go on. There is enough to cope with without adding the handicap of self-blame.

How you end your relationship with your employer often determines the kind of severance pay and other benefits you are given. Those who have a tendency to be more passive may be less likely to ask about what is due them, or to press for or even request benefits and assistance that exist but may not have been offered.

Women, for example, receive less outplacement assistance (job-search services paid for by your former employer) than men. This is probably because women are usually in lower positions, and outplacement tends to be more of an upper-management perk. But this is changing and women need to ask for outplacement assistance when they are laid off. Statistics from major outplacement firms indicate that companies are offering outplacement to lower levels of employees, thus, to more women. Drake Beam Morin reports that women now compose 25 percent of their clientele, up from 14 percent in 1988. Lee Hecht Harrison reports an increase of 37 percent from 27 percent, and at Challenger, Gray & Christmas, women now compose 10 percent of the client base, up from 5 percent in 1987.[24]

You should always ask what kind of outplacement assistance is available. If there isn't any, try to negotiate for some. Sometimes you'll get it just because you asked. Believe it or not, it may not have occurred to your employer to make it available to you.

It can also take longer for women to find jobs than men.

Lee Hecht Harrison found that it took its female clients 38 percent longer to find positions than male clients.[25] Some outplacement firms are adjusting their services to accommodate this added length of time.

Outplacement firms are also developing programs tailored to women's special needs. They are, for example, helping women conduct job searches that will not require relocation. Right Associates, an outplacement firm based in Philadelphia, has developed a new computerized system that can pinpoint potential employers in a defined geographical radius around their clients' homes.[26] Some firms even have special counseling sessions for "anchored" husbands (those who don't want to relocate for the wife's job), so that couples can discuss career options and sensitive issues like relocation. About 20 percent of American companies now offer job outplacement and a variety of relocation services for their transferred employees' "trailing spouses," and some, like the Impact Group in St. Louis, have special husband-oriented programs.[27]

Small-Company Opportunities

Smaller companies, where women can get hired more easily, have more responsibility, learn more and advance more quickly, are providing some of the better work opportunities. "The last place you'd expect to see quantifiable results is at a large corporation—it's far easier to achieve demonstrable change at smaller organizations," comments Judy Rosener.[28]

The advancement opportunity potential of small companies makes them very attractive to career-oriented women. Many of today's smaller companies will eventually become bigger companies making the Fortune 500 list in the year 2010 or even 2000, and a great number will have women at the helm. There are more than five million women heading up small- to medium-growth companies in the United States.[29] So today's middle manager in a small company could be tomorrow's CEO in a Fortune 500 company, or in a small- or medium-size company where the majority of this country's business growth is projected to take place—not a bad place to be if you want to move along in your career.

Women Entrepreneurs

There are many paths that lead women to become entrepreneurs. Some, pushed out of the corporate world, want to
run their own show, either in their current area of expertise
or in another field they are drawn to. Others opt for entrepreneurship as a way to have more control over balancing
work and family.

Current statistics show women are enjoying phenomenal
success in their entrepreneurial efforts. In 1992, they owned
6.5 million businesses. In 1991, women-owned businesses
accounted for 30 percent of all businesses in the United
States, up three times from 10 years ago, and employed 11
million people. In 1993, the National Foundation for Women
Business Owners estimated that the number of workers employed by women surpassed the number employed by the Fortune 500.[30] If this isn't clout, what is?

There are varying theories for why women are achieving
such success. One reason put forth is that women-owned
businesses tend to be stable and demonstrate even, slow
growth. Ironically, they are less in debt than men-owned companies, probably because fewer lenders are willing to finance
them.[31]

Some business analysts think their success is based on
so-called "female" personality traits, which encompass many
of the qualities needed to start and run a business: the ability to set realistic goals and juggle many tasks at once, a willingness to dig into detail and to admit when you don't know
how to do something, and the determination to then go out,
get the information and learn how to do it. Women will say,
"I'm not sure how to do this. But I can learn." And then they
do it.[32] These kinds of traits are invaluable to doing your own
thing, since the rigors and risks involved are sizable and require serious consideration. (See Chapter 9, Going On Your
Own.)

Pursuing Your Best Interests

In the long run, women *will* benefit from their sheer numbers and the needs of the American workplace. Since women compose 45 percent of the workforce in this country, companies that ignore almost half of the American workforce will be missing out on some great talent. "Listen up guys," says Charles Boesel, spokesman for the Women's Bureau at the U.S. Department of Labor. "You cannot cut out half the labor force and expect to be a successful corporation. If you want to retain the best and the brightest, you have to hire women . . . and have programs in place that keep them happy."[33]

At the same time, women should not rely on "winning by the numbers" for career opportunities and advancement. Like everyone, they need to be alert to opportunity. They also need to be *tactful and tireless self-promoters* to get ahead. It is still too easy for the work world to pass women by. Every woman must be responsible for managing her own career. If you want a promotion, ask for one. If you want to get ahead, plot out the necessary steps and take them.

A client of mine once received a very nice, but unexpected, promotion, moving from director to vice president. The new title and new responsibilities were carefully explained, but no one mentioned any increase in pay. After a week into her new position, she made a point to be in the office on a Saturday morning when she knew her boss usually came in to catch up on paperwork. Stopping by his office, she pleasantly said, "You know, Paul, this is a great opportunity for me and I'm really pleased you selected me for the vice-president position. But we haven't talked about my raise to go along with it." Believe it or not, Paul's response was, "Gosh, I hadn't thought about money." "I see," my client replied, "then let's think about it now." It wasn't the easiest sell, but three conversations and four days later she had a 20-percent raise to a salary commensurate with her new position.

There is no way of knowing if a man would have been offered the promotion *with* an accompanying raise, or if my client would have received one if she had waited. The important point is that it didn't matter because she went ahead and politely, but assertively, pursued her best interests. Women always need to proactively *take the next step*. It doesn't necessarily mean it will happen (it doesn't always happen for anyone), but your chances for success are a lot better than if you passively wait to see what fate will bring you.

PART FIVE:

REAL WORLD TACTICS

17. JOB SEARCH

I f you have read the previous chapters, you probably have a good understanding of what is happening in the workplace, how you fit or don't fit in it, and are ready to take the next, most important step: shifting from *thinking* to *doing*. It's easy to get stuck in the thinking stage, to want to have a clear course of action carefully plotted out before you target specific careers, prepare a résumé, or pick up the phone. Here's where many people get bogged down. They believe they must have it all figured out before they can take action.

Making a career move is a process, and it unfolds as you do it. It is also a learned skill and, as with any skill, there is a learning curve. The first career objective you pick or field you decide to explore may be exactly what you want to do. Or it may turn out to be a "thumbs-down" option that takes your thinking in a different direction. The first résumé or letter you write may be the one that lands you a great job, or it may be the third version that gets you employed. The single most important step you can take to get yourself moving in the right direction is to simply ***stop thinking and start acting***. Or, to borrow the famous Nike slogan, "Just do it."

Marketing Your "Imperfect Self"

Steady, unchanging careers are relics of the past. Everyone is making changes and will continue to do so. It's important to realize how this reality affects you and your job search. You are not likely to have a "seamless" work history with no employment gaps. Your education may not relate directly to your current focus. You may not have *any* experience in the field you want to enter. *All of this is okay.*

Do not get caught in the trap of thinking you are doomed because you don't have the "perfect background." Virtually no one has a perfect background. My clients often believe they will have a problem because they don't have a college degree, or their degree is in the "wrong" field. They say they don't have enough experience or too much at the wrong level. They fear they've changed jobs too many times or, if they have never changed jobs, are concerned people will wonder at their lack of ambition.

The list is endless—everyone can take something about themselves and turn it into a negative. *But these kinds of concerns are not career barriers, everyone is experiencing them.* Rather than stigmas, they have become common circumstances you and everyone must deal with as part of the job search, not fatal flaws that will stop you in your tracks.

Remember that everyone has his or her strengths and weaknesses. I've yet to meet the person who has the "right" degree in the "right" field, a seamless career history with steady promotions, and hasn't had a month or a year when his or her life came apart. The perfect job candidate does not exist—everyone has assets that help them sell themselves and liabilities they have to get around.

One of my former clients found herself widowed at 40. Her husband left no life insurance and they had very little savings. She had three small children under the age of six, no education beyond high school, and she hadn't worked since she was 20. Over the next five years, she held *14 different jobs*, often several simultaneously, doing everything from selling used cars to telemarketing credit cards to working a newspaper delivery route that got her up at 3:45 a.m. When I began working with her, she had gained a toe-hold in the insurance industry as a customer service representative and wanted to sell insurance. To say that writing her résumé was a challenge is an understatement. There is no résumé format that lets you easily explain 14 jobs in five years, or the circumstances behind them. But we managed. This woman had a lot of drive and determination and was dauntless. We turned her work history into an advantage by using it to illustrate how determined she was, how hard she worked and how quickly she learned. She landed a sales job with an insurance company, became their top producer and, two years ago, left to start her own agency. A success story against all odds.

Using Multiple Search Methods

One of the most frequently asked questions is, "What is *the* best job-search method to use?" While most people have some familiarity with basic job-search methods such as answering ads, networking, contacting companies directly or working with recruiters, they are often confused about which of these methods to use. This is a key concern; job seekers want to "get it right" and track down their next opportunity as quickly and efficiently as possible with a minimum of false starts, dead ends and inappropriate tactics.

There are thousands of sources to turn to for advice, and when you do, you will get thousands of different answers. *Everyone*, including close friends, the local automotive mechanic, as well as authors of the myriad of job-search books published, has a strong opinion on the right way to look for a job and will gladly share it with you. "You should always work with recruiters," someone will say. "Never work with recruiters," someone else will claim. "Send out at least 100 résumés in three weeks," a book will state. "Never answer ads, they are a waste of time," a magazine article will tell you. And each believes their method is the best.

My approach is to **use *all of the possible methods there are* to look for a job, because it is impossible to know in advance what is going to work.** It's like trying to second-guess fate. Some people get jobs through contacts or recruiters, some from "cold calling" on companies by identifying and approaching companies with a letter and phone call, and others from answering ads.

There is no way to know beforehand which option will bring you results, but the following overviews may help you put together your best strategy:

Answering Ads

Not many jobs are actually advertised, for example, or placed with recruiters. Since the mid-1980s, the number of new jobs advertised by employers has dropped almost 40 percent.[1] The ones that are advertised get hundreds (or thousands) of responses. The average ad in the *Wall Street Journal* was getting 2,000 to 3,000 responses in 1992. Clearly, the odds are not good.

When all occupations and industries are averaged together, less than 14 percent of the total number of jobs available are advertised.[2] If you want to include answering ads as part of your job search, put effort into finding all available ad sources. While local or regional newspapers are a logical source, don't neglect business publications, such as the *Wall Street Journal*, or the *National Business Employment Weekly* which lists all ads published in the *Wall Street Journal's* regional editions during the prior week. Look into trade journals specific to your industry or one you are exploring. Check *Professional's Job Finder, Non-Profits' Job Finder* and *Government Job Finder*, all of which list numerous ad sources, both by industry and geographic region and reference directories, newsletters and job telephone hot lines, as well.

Using Recruiters

Recruiters, or "headhunters" as they are sometimes called, are go-betweens or matchmakers for job seekers and hiring companies. While still popular, they are being used less today as companies try to fill positions in-house and save placement fees. Early in the 1990s recession, many recruiters who didn't close shop lost half their business but were still receiving as many as 50 to 100 unsolicited résumés a day.

If you plan to use recruiters, it helps to know how they work. They are paid a "placement fee" by the company doing the hiring—not the person being hired—to find qualified candidates to fill specific job openings. The fee is based on a percentage of the hired employee's first year's compensation, which can range anywhere from 15 to 40 percent, with 20 to 30 percent the average. The fee may be paid up front or in installments to see if the employee works out.

There are two kinds of recruiters: retained and contingency. A retained recruiter is the only one filling that specific job for that specific company (like a real estate agent with an exclusive property listing). Most recruiters work on a contingency basis where a hiring employer contacts multiple recruiters to find candidates to fill an opening. While all the recruiters may have potential candidates, only the one whose candidate is hired gets paid.

Good professional recruiters will level with you as to whether they think they can help you. They protect your confidentiality as well as the employer's and will describe you to the client without giving your name. Likewise, when recruiters tell you about an opportunity, initially they will not disclose the employer's identity. Names will be revealed only after they have checked with both parties and determined mutual interest.

With recruiters as a go-between, you have less control over the process, which can include: making the initial contact, overseeing the match-up, arranging interview logistics, even negotiating your compensation. On the other hand, you might not have landed in this employment situation were it not for the recruiter. So, it's a trade-off.

Networking and Prospecting

Between 70 percent and 85 percent of all jobs are "found" through less traditional methods like knowing someone in the company or by contacting companies directly.[3]

Networking: During the 1980s, books and articles advised developing and maintaining contacts at lunches, through professional groups, on airplanes, etc., on the theory that these relationships could help your career and make you a valuable contact for someone else, thus, part of their network.

Networking is still a valuable tool and you should make it part of your job-search strategy, but not your only tactic. Leads and jobs often come out of this process. Just don't be discouraged if people are friendly, but not helpful. It's usually a matter of timing and who they really know.

Important reminder: If you are networking while currently employed, determine who you can trust. Some people will be willfully or unknowingly indiscreet. There is nothing worse than going to work and having your boss say, "I hear you are thinking of leaving us."

In formulating your networking strategy, you may want to include attending meetings or conferences put on by professional organizations in your field or in one you want to enter. When you attend, don't try to snag people on the spot. Instead, get their card or find out where they work. Contact them a day or two after the meeting. It is far more courteous and may produce better results.

Prospecting: One of the most successful job-search strategies is prospecting, which means contacting a company executive in your area of expertise or interest through phone or letter regardless of whether or not you know they are hiring.

Prospecting is not to be confused with informational interviewing, no longer an appropriate tactic in today's job market. While the two are similar, the intent and approach differ. With informational interviewing, a much-emphasized job-search tactic in the 1970s and 1980s, job seekers called to set an hour interview with a company executive, said they were preparing for a possible job search and wanted information on a particular occupation or industry. With the workloads most people carry today, and the number of people in the job market, few have time to be interviewed, thus, the technique has lost its effectiveness.

By contrast, when you prospect, you present yourself by explaining you are looking for a position and would like to talk with them even if one isn't available. This is a subtle point, but an important one. The person you contact may have an opening, but may not want to tell you until he or she has met you and checked you out. By saying you want to talk regardless of openings, you get them off the hook. It works. Many of my clients have gone on prospecting interviews that turned into job interviews once the interviewer got to know them.

Doing It All

During a job search, a person might answer ads, prospect and conscientiously network with everyone he or she knows, but end up getting a job through a total stranger met in the doctor's office.

Given the unknowns, it is best to *try everything* and see where you get the best results. This approach gives you maximum flexibility. It allows you to cover all the bases *and* alter your strategies based on the feedback you get as you go along.

Using multiple job-search methods concurrently will speed you toward employment faster than using just one method at a time. For example, if you only answer ads for three weeks and don't see a lot of results, you haven't used those three weeks as effectively as you might have if you had been using multiple strategies. The rule here is: **The more you do, the quicker you will get there.** (See Afterword and Suggested Reading sections for resources to help you.)

The Importance of Putting Together a Good Résumé

During my 15 years in the corporate world, I directly hired or was involved in the hiring of a number of people and, consequently, read a lot of résumés. I remember the kinds of information I looked for, the frustration I felt reading hard-to-follow résumés, and the attitude I had when a résumé looked poorly produced or had typos. I also recall feeling respect and anticipation when I came upon a well-written one that caused me to want to interview the applicant.

A good résumé gives the reader just enough information in a format that makes sense. It presents currently important career data at the beginning and less important elements at the end. It begins by orienting the reader with a brief objective and then gives a brief summary of your strong points. It describes your work history with narrative statements, but also includes the company names, the cities where you worked and the dates for each job (in years, not months). It summarizes your education and training and includes often overlooked but relevant information like continuing-education courses, seminars, or licenses and certificates. It omits information not vital to the situation; i.e., you enjoy fishing or are captain of your bowling team. And it doesn't lie.

Truth and Honesty

Tell the truth. "Everything on your résumé must be defendable and discussible," says Peter Thorpe, a vice president at Citibank. "If you list stamp collecting as an interest, somewhere down the line you're going to run into a philatelist."[4]

Not telling the truth can catch up with you. "Companies are verifying résumés and applications more thoroughly than they have in the past, partly because more people are stretching the truth in order to compete for jobs in today's depressed market," says Beckie Harris, manager of staffing and employment at Ameritech Information Systems.[5] There is less need to cloud information since former "problems," like employment gaps, are common now and don't have to be concealed.

Be aware that you may be asked to provide proof of academic degrees, job titles, dates of employment, even college grade point averages. And virtually every employment application has the disclaimer, "I swear this information is true and complete to the best of my knowledge and belief." When you sign one, you are accountable for what you have stated.

Even though they may not have requested it before, some companies, on your first day of employment, will ask for authorization to contact your former employer to verify your salary or other data at your last job. If what they are told doesn't check out with what you said, you can be dismissed.

Ultimately, what you say in your résumé is up to you, but keep in mind that it's not worth going through all the effort of a job search only to lose a position or an opportunity because you misrepresented yourself.

What Should **Not** *Go Into Your Résumé*

Don't include your age, sex, marital status, health condition or other personal data in your résumé. Most organizations cannot legally request this information; besides, no one has ever said they were in poor health or unhappily married. And for every person who may think it's great that you have three kids, there may be another who belongs to a zero-population-growth organization and will decide you are irresponsible.

Omit interests and hobbies unless they are *really relevant to your career goals*. You may be a whiz on the golf course, but the reader of your résumé may hate golf. Applicants have even been screened out because they listed that they skied, and prospective employers were worried they would take excessive time off or get injured.

Reactions like this may not be well-founded, or even rational, but the reality is that they do occur, and you do yourself a disservice by taking a needless risk. It's better to leave off potentially controversial information than to eliminate yourself from an opportunity over something that isn't relevant or anyone's business to begin with.

Don't use a valuable line of space on your résumé with the statement, "References furnished upon request." It's assumed that everyone has references they can produce when asked. No one has ever stated "I do not have any references" on his or her résumé.

Remembering the Purpose of Your Résumé

Think of your résumé as a "career picture" and take the same care in crafting it as you would in preparing for an important personal photo session. Your résumé gives a quick picture of your career, and says something about you by its appearance and presentation. Like a picture, it doesn't tell everything—but what it does reveal needs to be crisp, sharp, focused and flattering, while remaining true to reality.

If you're not clear about the mechanics of creating your own résumé, you can find good resources in the Afterword and Suggested Reading sections that will help you.

How Long Will It Take?

Every job seeker asks, "How long will it take me to find my next job?" ***"Longer than you think it will,"*** is usually what I tell my clients. This isn't being cruel, it's being realistic. No one wants to hear it can take a long time. There is always the occasional miraculous story of someone being hired the day after being laid off, or of individuals making money only two months after leaving their former company and starting their own business. But these are "miracles," not the norm.

Finding a new job opportunity has always taken time. In today's workplace, it is taking even longer. The rule of thumb used to be that for every $10,000 of salary you wanted, add a month to your job search. Now some experts advise doubling this. In the best of times, it took an average of three months to find a management position; now it takes six. And, in a field with high unemployment or in a high-salary range ($100,000 and up), it can easily take a year or more.[6]

Remember, these are average statistics, not predestined outcomes. Every person is different. Some rapid-success factors are out of your control. You may be exiting a vanishing industry, or live in a particularly depressed local economy.

The interviewing process itself may take a while. Multiple interviews are standard for people in upper-management positions and have now extended to most levels. You may find yourself interviewing with potential peers, heads of other key departments, and even possible subordinates in addition to the person you would actually report to. Have patience. While these delays may make you feel out of control, remember that other factors, like your attitude and how much effort you put into the job search, *are in your control and do make a difference.*

The Amount of Effort Required

After working with clients, reflecting on my own career, and observing those of family and friends, I firmly believe that the most important factor in determining the length of a job search is *how much* effort is put into it.

Most people don't realize the sheer amount of effort and persistence it takes to find their next career opportunity. "Well, I answered some ads," they say. "And I talked to a recruiter and I called the people I know really well in my industry. I've looked, I didn't find anything, and now I don't know what to do." It usually takes much more effort than this. Jeff Barton,* 45, a former field manager of a chain of 210 retail clothing stores put considerable effort into his five-month search. In a typical week he made 50 to 75 phone calls, wrote 20 to 40 letters, networked like crazy and scrutinized the job ads. But all this intense activity paid off when he landed a position as an Eastern-states regional sales manager for another retailer.[7]

Your required level of effort may depend on your particular circumstances and goals, such as if you have just been laid off and need to find work as soon as possible or are in a comfortable employment situation which allows you to leisurely explore different opportunities, or if you are just returning to work after an absence from the job market.

Each of these scenarios presents its own advantages and drawbacks. If you are currently working, you may feel less pressure to find a new job, but discover it's harder to find the time and motivation to conduct your search. If you are not working, you may have a lot of time to look, but feel the pressure of needing to find something as quickly as possible.

To help decide realistically what you can do, set goals initially for a week or two at the most and see how you do. At the end of the week make an assessment: Did you plan too much? Or did you have a lot of time left over that you could have filled with other job-search tasks?

Being Realistic About How You Use Your Time

There are many who feel that if you are not working, you should be looking for work eight hours a day, every day. Personally, I don't think there is enough to do on a daily basis to make job search a full-time job. Things take time. Between the pace of the average business day, playing phone tag and accommodating other people's availability, there is only so much you can do in one day. Sometimes, phone calls and an interview can take up the entire day. On other days, you may be done with your letters, phone calls and research by 10:30 a.m. How do you deal with this? **Plan on doing some job-search task *every* day, but don't expect that it will always take *all* day to do it.** Do it first, and tell yourself you can't do anything else until you are done. Don't try to economize your time and cram all your job hunting into two days a week and do nothing the other three. You won't get enough done and you won't stay focused. Instead, plan to do something *every* day, with an occasional day off.

When you are done for the day, tell yourself you are free to do something else. Plan your "free time" as carefully as you do your job-search time. This can be a good opportunity to take a class to increase your computer literacy, finish a long-postponed home-improvement project or even take up a new hobby. (It *is* okay to have some fun during this time.) Although it can be hard when you are used to having your day structured by work, you must take responsibility for the "loose" hours you will have each day. Otherwise, you can end up bored, depressed and in your bathrobe, which won't help your morale and will adversely affect your job-search efforts.

It's tedious, but each bit of effort is what will eventually get you there. James Challenger, president of outplacement firm Challenger, Gray & Christmas, boils it down to the basics: "There is no secret to getting jobs; it all depends on the number of interviews you've been to. . . . All you have to do is get across the desk from someone who thinks like you do and you've got a shot at a job. But people tend to sit at home and wait for somebody to call them."[8] *Consistency* and *persistence* should be your watchwords. They will pay off.

Don't Stop Until It's Over

If you are a basketball fan, you know it's one game where "it's not over till it's over." The game is played for 48 minutes, but often can go either way in the final five minutes or even five seconds. Professional basketball players know that even when their team is 10 points ahead with two minutes to go, they can't let up their effort or intensity until the final buzzer rings and the game is over.

Job search is a lot like basketball. You shouldn't stop your search until you've been hired (or have made a definitive, well-informed decision to start your own venture). "Being hired" is defined as being offered and having accepted a position, with all the terms worked out and a firm starting date. Preferably, all in writing. Anything less may mean you have not actually been hired. And until you are, in fact, hired, you must keep looking, even if you are "sure" you are going to get it.

Even very firm situations can unravel in the "final few minutes of the game." Allen Jacobs* was contacted by a recruiter about an interesting job opportunity to create a new division for a national direct marketing company. Although employed, Allen was interested. Over the next six weeks, Allen had seven interviews, two out-of-state, with the company flying him in to interview with personnel at different facilities. In the seventh interview, Allen and the company president negotiated salary and talked about a start date. But then the whole thing evaporated. Suddenly everything stalled, and phone calls went unanswered. Finally, the company said it needed some time to "figure things out." Two months later, the recruiter called Allen and told him the company had decided not to start the new division, which meant they wouldn't be hiring anyone.

This is not an unusual situation, unfortunately. While most circumstances may not involve such extensive interviewing, it is not uncommon for promising situations to suddenly come apart. This is especially true in today's workplace, where corporate decisions are often in flux, and a company's circumstances or plans can change rapidly. "Jobs will just disappear. A company will decide to hire somebody, and then they just don't," said Meg Forester,* a 36-year-old finance executive whose hot job prospect disappeared. (But she was hired by another firm eight months later).[9]

Worse than the "sure-shot" situation is the "imaginary sure shot," when people identify an opportunity, independently decide they will definitely get the job and stop looking further. This can occur after one interview, when they were told they will be notified *if* they make it to the next round, or when they have simply answered an ad and may not have even gotten a response, but unreasonably decide it's just a matter of waiting until the offer comes in. In these situations, the sense of false certainty is rooted in "wishing it were so." It happens because anxiety and the discomfort of looking for a job cause people to become overly optimistic and to treat their hopes as realities.

Don't get caught in these it's-in-the-bag traps, real or imaginary. If you have had one interview, that's great, but keep looking. If you are one of two final candidates for a position, that's even better, but keep looking. Don't stop your search efforts until you have a job. This is one time when it is really true that "it's not over till it's over."

Getting Help

Looking to outside help to assist in your job search can be a good idea. A good book or two can help you formulate a sound job-search plan. A qualified counselor or support group can help initiate your search, keep you motivated and give you a safe place to let off steam from the pressures of the task. Just be careful about how you select outside help since your time and money are particularly precious commodities at this time.

Books, Tapes and Computer Programs

There are many books written on the logistics of job search, as well as computer programs, audio tapes and video tapes. To find the better ones, check to see how recently they have been published or updated. A good resource is one that is geared towards the current job market. The workplace has recently changed so dramatically that job-search methods effective even three years ago may not work now.

Choosing a Career Counselor

Much advice has been written about how to find a good career counselor. Many excellent sources may be helpful.

Be aware that career counseling is not a regulated profession. Once you've selected a reputable person, be sure the chemistry is good. A good rapport, in work style and personality, must exist if the relationship is going to work well.

Seeking Out Support Groups

A support group can give you direction, reinforce your confidence and provide comfort from others in the same situation. "I was floundering like a fish out of water [before joining]," said one support group participant, "There's nothing better than being with people in your situation. I mean, here is a place where it's safe to talk. . . ." "People actually share information," another group member remarked. "They go out on interviews and then come back and brief others who have subsequent interviews."[10]

Some excellent support groups are sponsored through state unemployment programs. In Orange County, California, for example, the Employment Development Department (EDD) program offers two good programs: the Professional Employment Network in Santa Ana and Success Plus in Garden Grove. Both lead job seekers through the entire process, from focusing on an objective, to developing résumés and letters, to interviewing. They also provide office facilities, including word processing and phone lines, which are free to participants. Rather than paying money, group members volunteer a specific number of hours each week as program staff, with guidance from the EDD personnel.

There are also privately offered support groups. The Five O'Clock Club, founded by Kate Wendleton, originated in New York and has expanded into New Jersey, Louisiana, Philadelphia, Massachusetts, Connecticut and Texas.[11] They offer job search/strategy support sessions headed by professional counselors, meet weekly and charge $40 for a two-hour session.[12] Forty Plus, a support group for individuals 40 years of age and older with salaries at $40,000+, charges low fees but requires active participation. It is totally participant-managed, and all members work at the group's facility a certain number of hours each week as long as they are in the group. Forty Plus provides a full range of job-search support as well as office facilities and a telephone answering service. Check out your local employment office, library or phone book to locate government and privately sponsored groups available in your community.

Taking Advantage of Outplacement Opportunities

If you are laid off, your company may offer you "outplacement services," job-search counseling *paid for by your employer*. Outplacement services can include one-on-one counseling and temporary office space use or group seminars and workshops. Always take advantage of any outplacement programs available to you. The kind of service you receive may depend on your ranking in the company, with higher-level employees getting the more expensive, personalized offerings. But, in any case, outplacement can be a valuable resource and it doesn't cost you anything.

Beware of Scams and Rip-Offs

One of the unfortunate results of the tightened job market is an increase in fraudulent career and job-search services. "There is a great potential to defraud people who are desperate for a job," reports Rosemarie Bonta of the Miami Better Business Bureau.[13] A 1991 poll by the National Consumer League revealed that job seekers lost $15 billion on job-search scams and rip-offs.[14]

The most common rip-offs are agencies that promise to "tap the hidden job market," "guarantee" jobs and require large fees paid in advance for their services. Often, these agencies will claim to have exclusive job leads or databases that match clients with an exclusive source of job opportunities. Their fees run high, usually based on how much you were earning. They are shameless about finding out your salary level before stating their fees. Many will even hand you a questionnaire asking details not only of your professional life, but also queries about your family and finances, including savings accounts, real estate and credit-card debt. Then, based on your responses, they will quote you a fee for "someone at your level." Prices can range from $2,000 to $30,000+. All or part must be paid up-front, and some agencies will happily provide financing.

Overall, results and services tend to be poor or non-existent once a client enters the program. Supposedly "hot job leads" can turn out to be photocopied lists of companies from outdated directories. Résumés can be sloppily produced documents taken from slightly altered "boiler-plate" formats used for everyone. In Washington, D.C., an agency promised job-strategy assistance plus 20 new leads a week in its client's field, human resources, for a fee of $485. The results? A print-out of all the D.C. government jobs and leads for entry-level positions in data processing. In Phoenix, a corporate-training consultant borrowed $3,500 from her father to pay a firm promising employment in six weeks. She was dismayed when she received a computer-generated list of 100 job openings, of which 30 were repeats. Worse yet, after calling, she discovered more than half of the companies were no longer in business. In fact, only 20 firms still existed and none had any openings.[15]

While it seems incredible that anyone would buy into these scams, lots of very smart people get taken in. The personnel in these agencies are great salespeople who know that job seekers are often panicky, unfamiliar with how to look for a job and all too willing to believe there is a "quick fix." "They got me at a weak moment," says an otherwise savvy political appointee who paid $4,700 in advance for shoddy services. "I was so down on myself that I figured I could use a little outside help."[16]

Beware of classified ads that promise high-paying jobs and advertise an 800 number. The call will often result in a request for up-front money for a "starter kit," which usually turns out to be general information about the company. Or the 800 number may refer you to a 900 number for additional information. The 900 number is not free, you pay by the minute. In either case, you are laying out money and not getting job leads or interviews in return. Ads like this may even offer free training, guaranteed job placement or government grants to lure customers.[17]

Another ploy is classified ads that advertise job opportunities overseas, promising paid travel, housing, medical expenses and high salaries. Respondents are referred to pay-per-call phone lines or asked for up-front "job listings" fees. The listings, if they are even sent, may include outdated classified ads from the area and, perhaps, some travel brochures. One scam had job seekers sending in $99 or more to receive information about living conditions in Australia and lists of companies "looking for employees." The companies were not looking for workers. According to the Australian Embassy in Washington, D.C., Australia was in a serious recession and had 11 percent unemployment when these ads were run. Another rip-off.[18]

A Word About Career Testing

Many job seekers wonder about the benefits of career testing. The decision to take career tests is an individual one, but there are some points to consider before you make up your mind.

First, understand what the test is measuring and what the results will tell you. Some tests, like the well-known Myers-Briggs, will define your personality type based on its particular system. Other tests, like the Strong-Campbell Interest Inventory, will measure your interest in a variety of career areas, but not your aptitude. Some are designed by the individual or firm offering them. Before signing up, be sure that the purpose, methodology and results of such tests are adequately explained and that you understand how the results will be useful to you. Be aware that testing is not a sure-fire solution to figuring out what to do. Personality-type information is useful, but doesn't necessarily point to specific career choices. Interests are good to know, but you also need to have an aptitude for them. (A client of mine would love to be a woodworker, but is woefully lacking in manual dexterity.) Aptitude can tell you a lot, but you can be good at something and still dislike it. (A salesperson may confirm that he or she is great at sales, even though burned-out with the career.)

If you do opt for career testing, shop around. Prices can vary from $50 to over $1,000, with $200 to $400 not being uncommon. Try to find a qualified individual or firm offering a fair price. And when you get the results, use them to augment what you already know about yourself. Pay attention if the results don't seem to fit. You don't want to make life decisions based on faulty or inappropriate data.

How to "Just Do It"

When you begin your job search, you may feel like you are in a "Catch 22" situation: You can't decide on what you want to do until you start looking into it, but you don't see how you can look into something if you are not sure it is really what you want to do. The way out of this decision-making loop is to recognize that you don't have to be sure before you can begin. **It's okay to start your job search without being positive you have selected the perfect goal.** You can start with one objective, decide it's not the one for you and change it. In fact, flexibility is a key factor in figuring out where it is you want to go and getting there.

However, when you pursue a new field or occupation, *you must be able to explain the reasoning that led you to choose the new direction,* even though, privately, you are not sure if this is your ultimate goal. You must communicate your reasoning in your résumé, your letters, your conversations and your interviews. Do not expect people to understand your logic if you don't spell it out for them. You must tell them why your goals make sense. The rule is: ***Make it clear.***

Jasper Witton* had been an auditor for 11 years with a large accounting firm. During this time, he acquired a lot of experience working with computer systems and found he liked the "computer" aspect of his job the most. When hard times hit and Jasper was laid off, he decided his next job would be in the computer industry. But he was not clear on the specifics or even sure he could make the switch. He didn't know what kind of position to look for in the computer industry. He did know he did not have a "classic" computer background and that his choice would be questioned—Why was he leaving accounting where he had a firm background to go into a field where he had no formal education or work history?

While uncertain of how he would fit, Jasper did understand the thinking and feelings that had brought him to this choice. As a result, he was able to:

- Clearly explain how he had become involved with computers.
- Give specific examples of the experience he had obtained.

- Show how his background was relevant, although non-traditional.
- Demonstrate that his interest was genuine and based on his experiences.

Jasper worked hard at communicating these points in all aspects of his job search. It wasn't an overnight victory, but he eventually found a position as a member of a user support team for a software provider that specialized in accounting systems.

Reality-Testing

What Jasper did is called **reality-testing**. He had an idea, created a hypothesis, and got out and tested it in the real world. *Reality-testing* is what helps you make a series of informed decisions that ultimately lead to your next career objective. You can collect a great deal of information before you actually start looking for a job. You can take career tests, consult with career counselors, read books, and go to classes and seminars. While these are valuable first steps, they aren't the whole process. **You have to get out in the real world and test your information to see if it is valid.**

When you reality-test, pay close attention to feedback. If the first or second person you talk to says, "I really can't see you making that kind of change," consider what they have to say, but don't quit yet. If you go on to talk to five people who say the same thing, then it's possible they are right. This is the reality-test you are looking for. At the same time, check your presentation. Are you presenting yourself correctly by showing all of the reasons why the change makes sense? Are you leaving anything out of your experience, or is a particular aspect of your experience being misunderstood?

Kathy Garcia* sold office supplies for five years and was one of the top three producers in her company nationwide. But when her sales became severely impacted by suppliers selling directly to the public, Kathy decided she wanted to stay in sales, but leave her shrinking industry. She targeted pharmaceutical sales, which she knew was a growing area. But after a few phone conversations and informal interviews, Kathy discovered the large pharmaceutical companies preferred to hire recent college graduates who could be trained "their way" from the start, uninfluenced by prior sales training and experience. This was something Kathy couldn't change. Instead, she had to alter her career objective. After more research, she targeted retail wholesalers of over-the-counter drugs and sundries who wanted experienced sales representatives and welcomed her strong background.

It's a Numbers Game

Approach your search as a numbers game. "A job search is essentially about numbers," says outplacement specialist James Challenger. "You have to make a lot of calls and sweat through a lot of interviews. . . . The more people you see, the quicker you're going to get a position."[19]

It is exactly like sales. A salesperson must make numerous phone calls to get one sale. You are in precisely the same position; you need to include a batch of companies in your search. Realize that you don't really know what a company is up to unless you talk to someone there. Businesses launch new products, change computer systems or make other kinds of changes that might lead to a job opportunity. But often these changes are not made known to the public.

Leo Guardian* was a training specialist. When he began his job search, he focused on large companies because he thought they were more likely to have training departments than smaller companies. After contacting six large companies in his area and finding no openings, Leo was discouraged. He decided to take a new approach and started thinking about what kinds of companies would need trainers based on their products or services, not their size. Some financial services companies, he discovered, need to provide ongoing product, sales and customer support training to their employees to keep up with product changes and maintain their customer base. So Leo started contacting them, regardless of their size, even if he didn't know anything about the company. His efforts paid off. After running through two dozen financial service firms of all sizes in his city, he found an opportunity as a staff trainer with a pension services administration company.

One of the factors that led Leo to successfully locating a position is that he *learned not to pre-qualify or disqualify companies from his search if he didn't know anything about them*. If Leo tried to research a company and couldn't find out anything about them, he still included them in his job search and contacted them. This is an important concept: **Don't get caught in the research myth**.

The Research Myth

Traditionally, career wisdom has had job seekers thoroughly researching each company they planned to contact. A challenging task, since often there is little information available about the average locally based company. Insight on large companies is not always readily obtainable either. While the library may have general information on large companies, there are often few details about individual business units. Newspapers and trade journals may carry some news if something really good or bad happens to a company.

Contrary to previous advice you may have received, if you don't know anything about a company, don't let lack of information stop you. Contact it anyway. If you do get a response, you are that much ahead. If you're asked why you contacted them without knowing anything about them, explain the situation. Tell them that you tried, couldn't find anything, but wanted to include them in your efforts because you are conducting a very extensive search in your determination to find a position. Rather than chiding you for not having specific information, people will be impressed with your persistence and courage.

This is one of those times that "nothing ventured, nothing gained" definitely applies. Besides, after you talk to the company, you will know something about it and, consequently, something about other companies like it. Don't bog down over a lack of information and never let that be an excuse to halt or slow-start your job search. Instead, *create your own database —it's recent, firsthand and specific to your job search.*

The I'm-The-Answer-To-Your-Problems Mistake

If you do find information about a company, use it judiciously. **Don't assume you know everything about the company and present yourself as the only one who can solve its problems.** This approach can backfire.

Even with inside information, it is presumptuous to think you know enough about a company to actually develop useful solutions to their problems from the outside. Situations may exist that are unknown to outsiders. Or a particular company may be the exception to the rule in its industry and not have the problems tearing its competitors apart.

Because you don't really know what is going on, or what is needed, the "I-can-solve-your-problems" approach can be plainly arrogant. Most business people don't react well to receiving letters that say, "I know what is wrong with your company and I can fix it." Instead, their responses may be, "Who does this person think he is? If it could be fixed, we'd have fixed it" or "This doesn't describe our situation. Obviously this person knows nothing about what is really going on here, even though she thinks she does." Such approaches do not make favorable impressions.

It is okay to show that you are aware of industrywide situations or even particular problems if they are very public, and that someone with your background could be valuable. But don't take the hard-sell, "I'm-the-one-to-lead-you-out-of-the-desert" approach.

The I-Only-Want-To-Work-Here Mistake

Some people will have their hearts set on working for a particular company and devote their job-search efforts to it.

The geography may be perfect, or the company is identical to the one they left or is a leader in the field they want to enter.

Don't pursue your dream company exclusively. Focusing on just one company is like putting all your eggs in one basket, a bad strategy. No matter how good the fit, there's a strong chance someone with your talents is not needed at the moment, no matter how great these talents are. If you do get in, that's great. But if you don't, you need to have other strategies going at the same time so a minimum of effort and time will be wasted.

The Story on "Hot" Careers

Every year forecasts are put out by *Working Woman, Working Mother, U.S. News & World Report* and other publications identifying what occupations and industries will be "hot" in terms of growth and new-job creation. Over the next 15 years, for example, the health care and human services industries are predicted to expand by more than 70 percent.[20] Computer and data processing services are considered major growth areas.[21] The service sector is expected to account for almost half of all new positions created by 2005.[22]

While information about "hot" careers is useful, two factors should be used in evaluating it. One is the reason a field or occupation is being defined as "hot." The other is how relevant a "hot" field is to you personally.

The restaurant industry, for example, is a growing service industry. But many of the jobs that it creates will be in food preparation and service. The "hot" criteria here is the *number of jobs* that may be created, not the caliber of jobs in terms of pay or career growth. At the opposite end of the spectrum, pharmacy is a "hot" occupation, both in terms of the number of positions and salary. But the feasibility of becoming a pharmacist depends on your willingness and ability to get the necessary education.

The point here is not to bash any given occupation or propose that one is better than another. Rather, "hot" opportunities need to be evaluated in the context of your own circumstances. Do you want to go back to school? Are there growth-industry companies located in your area? Are you willing to relocate? While the criteria will vary from person to person, everyone needs to weigh what an area of opportunity means to them. A career may be "hot" statistically, but you need to decide if it is "hot" *for you personally.*

A Cyclical Process

The success of your job search really depends on you. You must do everything you can, as well as you can, and not stop until you have secured a position. Armed with the best job-search knowledge possible, you can move forward with optimism and determination.

Once you land your next position, give it all you've got. But don't expect that it will be the last of your career moves. Most Americans will hold a variety of jobs in more than one field during their working life. We are living longer and will be working longer. Changes will continually reshape the workplace, which means you may have to relearn—or at least update—the job-search process each time you make a career move. Today's successful search strategies are not the same ones effective prior to the 1990-1991 recession.

It is your responsibility to stay current and adjust your tactics to successfully maneuver each turn in the path of your working life. In fact, your primary job is to actively manage your career. "We've broken the whole mommy and daddy syndrome," says outplacement expert William Morin. "Nobody else is responsible for your happiness. You have to see yourself as a business. That is your job."[23]

How you approach the twists and turns in your career will mean the difference between handling them with a comfortable anticipation of the unknown or confronting them with a sense of dread and a fear of what lurks around the next corner. Attitude counts considerably here so you must think as positively as you can. Barry Bauling, a savvy marketing executive and perhaps the most successful person I know at facing life with a good attitude, says, "There is no way to go but forward."

Forward is always a good direction, especially when you are not quite sure how to proceed. Move with confidence toward the unknown. It's the best way to get there.

---

* *Names and some details have been changed.*

PART SIX:

AFTERWORD: WHAT DO I DO NEXT?

AFTERWORD: WHAT DO I DO NEXT?

A Few Words from the Author . . .

Dear Readers:

I hope this book has helped you formulate a plan for managing your career. If I were to have you take away one thought, it would be that you must think of your career as your business and manage all facets of it accordingly. That is the path to success in today's changing workplace.

By reading this book, you have already started a new journey:

- You now know more than most of the people you will be competing with for jobs and career moves.

- You can move forward with enough information about the working world to help you make informed choices and good decisions.

- You're less likely to be surprised by changes in the workplace and you're better prepared to deal with them.

- You can be more proactive as you look ahead and plan your next steps.

There are certain tools you'll need to put your plan into action. In the Suggested Reading section I have listed some excellent resources that can help you create your résumé, develop job-search tactics and hone your interviewing skills.

I've also created the "What Do I Do Now? Tool Kit," which details my most successful techniques to help you:

- Tailor a job-search plan to your particular situation.
- Create a résumé that's effective and will stand out from the rest.
- Draft letters to answer ads, set up prospecting and job interviews, network and follow up on opportunities.
- Bring your interviewing skills up-to-date so you can make every interview count.
- Skillfully negotiate salaries and benefits.

An order form for the Tool Kit is at the back of this book.

Please contact me if you have questions. And in early 1995, watch for my next book, titled, *What Do I Do Now? Effective Management Tools for the New Workplace.*

All of us face a complex and changing workplace. While the going may seem rough, I firmly believe that knowledge, faith and determination will get you through.

My sincere wishes for career success,

Shena Crane
c/o Vista Press
2102 Business Center Drive
Irvine, CA 92715
714/497-9811

PART SEVEN:

SUGGESTED READING

SUGGESTED READING

Recommended Resources for Career Development and Planning, Job Search, Résumés, Letters and Interviewing

These books will assist you with the complete job-search process, including skills and interests assessments, job-search planning, résumés, letters and interviewing:

Mary Lindley Burton and Richard A. Wedemeyer, *In Transition— From the Harvard Business School Club of New York's Career Management Seminar*, New York: HarperCollins Publishers, 1991

Geraldine Henze, *Winning Career Moves—A Complete Job Search Program for Managers and Professionals*, Illinois: Business One Irwin, 1992

Barrie Hopson and Mike Scally, *Build Your Own Rainbow—A Workbook for Career & Life Management*, San Diego, California: Pfeiffer & Company, 1993

Tom Jackson, *Not Just Another Job*, New York: Times Books, 1992

Dr. Ronald L. Krannich, *Careering and Re-Careering for the '90s: Skills and Strategies for Shaping Your Future*, Monases Park, Virginia: Impact Publications, 1993

Dorothy Leeds, *Marketing Yourself: The Ultimate Job Seeker's Guide*, New York: HarperCollins Publishers, 1991

Charles H. Logue, Ph.D., *Outplace Yourself—Secrets of an Executive Outplacement Counselor*, Massachusetts: Bob Adams, Inc., 1993

Tom Morton, *The Survivors Guide to Unemployment*, Colorado: Pinon Press, 1992

Kate Wendleton, *Through The Brick Wall: How to Job-Hunt in a Tight Market*, New York: Villard Books, 1992

Martin Yate, *Knock 'Em Dead—The Ultimate Job Seeker's Handbook*, Massachusetts: Bob Adams, Inc., 1993

If you're writing your own résumé, look at these books:

Richard H. Beatty, *The Resume Kit*, New York: John Wiley & Sons, 2nd Edition, 1991

Ronald L. Krannich and Caryl Rae Krannich, Ph.D.s, *Dynamite Résumés & 101 Great Examples and Tips for Success*, Virginia: Impact Publishing, 1992

Yana Parker, *The Damn Good Resume Book*, Berkeley, California: Ten Speed Press, 1989

Yana Parker, *The Resume Catalog: 2000 Damn Good Examples*, Berkeley, California: Ten Speed Press, 1988

Check out these resources to help you develop cover letters:

Richard H. Beatty, *175 High Impact Cover Letters*, New York: John Wiley & Sons, Inc., 1992

William S. Frank, *200 Letters for Job Hunters*, Berkeley, California: Ten Speed Press, 1990

Ronald L. Krannich and Caryl Rae Krannich, Ph.D.s, *Dynamite Cover Letters and Other Great Job Search Letters*, Virginia: Impact Publishing, 1992

Use these to brush up on your interviewing skills:

Deborah P. Bloch, *How to Have a Winning Job Interview*, Lincoln, Illinois: VGM Career Horizons, 1992

John Caple, Ph.D., *The Ultimate Interview*, New York: Doubleday Dell Publishing Group, Inc., 1991

David R. Eyler, *Job Interviews That Mean Business*, New York: Random House, 1992

Ron Fry, *101 Great Answers to the Toughest Interview Questions*, Hawthorne, New Jersey: The Career Press, 1991

Research careers, industries, jobs and companies using these resources:

Karmen Crowthner, *Researching Your Way to a Good Job— How to Find and Use Information on Industries, Companies, Jobs, Careers*, New York: John Wiley & Sons, Inc., 1993

Daniel Lauber, *Professional's Job Finder*, River Forest, Illinois: Planning Communications, 1992

Daniel Lauber, *Non-Profits' Job Finder*, River Forest, Illinois: Planning Communications, 1992

Daniel, Lauber, *Government Job Finder*, River Forest, Illinois: Planning Communications, 1992

Robert O. Snellings, Sr., *Jobs! What They Are . . . Where They Are . . . What They Pay!*, New York: Simon & Schuster, 1992

John W. Wright, *Where The Jobs Are*, New York: Avon Books, 1992

The following are for special groups and situations:

College Graduates:

Ron Fry, *Your First Interview—For College Students and Anyone Preparing to Enter Today's Tough Job Market*, Hawthorne, New Jersey: The Career Press, 1993

Ron Fry, *Your First Résumé—A Comprehensive Guide for College Students or Anyone Preparing to Enter or Reenter the Job Market*, Hawthorne, New Jersey: Career Press, 1992

Joyce Lain Kennedy and Dr. Darryl Laramore, *Joyce Lain Kennedy's Career Book*, Illinois: VGM Career Horizons— NTC Publishing Group, 1993

Dorothy Rogers and Craig Betinson, *How to Market Your College Degree*, Illinois: VGM Career Horizons—NTC Publishing Group, 1992

Entrepreneurship / Working at Home:

Jane Applegate, *Succeeding in Small Business—The 101 Toughest Problems and How to Solve Them*, New York: Penguin Books USA, Inc., 1992

Lynie Arden, *The Work at Home Sourcebook*, Boulder, Colorado: Live Oak Publications, 1992

Minorities:

Floyd Dickens, Jr., *The Black Manager, Making It In The Corporate World*, New York: AMACOM, 1991

Michael F. Kastre, Nydia Kastre, and Alfred G. Edwards, *The Minority Career Guide—What African Americans, Hispanics, and Asian Americans Must Know to Succeed in Corporate America*, Princeton, New Jersey: Peterson's, 1993

Miquela Rivera, Ph.D., *The Minority Career Book*, Massachusetts: Bob Adams, Inc., 1991

R. Roosevelt Thomas, Jr., *Beyond Race and Gender— Unleashing the Power of Your Total Work Force by Managing Diversity*, New York: AMACOM, 1991

Disabled Workers:

Melanie Astaire Witt, *Job Strategies for People With Disabilities*, Princeton, New Jersey: Peterson's Guides, 1992

Military Personnel:

D. F. Reardon, Ph.D., *In or Out of the Military: How to Make Your Own Best Decision*, Oak Harbor, Washington: Pepper Press, 1993

Temporary Work:

Karen Mendenhall, *Making the Most of the Temporary Employment Market*, Ohio: Betterway Books, 1993

Older Workers:

J. Robert Connor, *Cracking the Over-50 Job Market*, New York: Penguin Books USA, 1992

Ken Dychtwald, Ph.D. and Joe Flower, *Age Wave—How the Most Important Trend of Our Time Will Change Your Future*, New York: Bantam Books, 1990

Women:

Patricia Aburdene & John Naisbitt, *Megatrends for Women*, New York: Villard Books, 1992

Janet Hauter, *The Smart Women's Guide to Career Success*, New Jersey: Career Press, 1993

Michelle Jackman with Susan Waggoner, *Successful Career Strategies for Women in the 1990's—Star Teams, Key Players*, New York: Ballantine Books, 1991

Julie Adair King, *The Smart Woman's Guide to Interviewing and Salary Negotiation*, New Jersey: Career Press, 1993

Jane White, *A Few Good Women—Breaking the Barriers to Top Management*, New Jersey: Prentice Hall, 1992

PART EIGHT:

FOOTNOTES

*F*OOTNOTES

Chapter 1

[1]   Sources for impact on white-collar and blue-collar workers from: (1) David Hage, Linda Grant, Jim Impoco, "White Collar Wasteland," *U.S. News & World Report*, June 28, 1993, 42; (2) Erica L. Groshen, Donald Williams, "White- and Blue-Collar Jobs in the Recent Recession and Recovery: Who's Singing the Blues?," *Economic Review*, Fourth Quarter, 1993, 1-11; (3) Thomas Nardone, Diane Herz, Steven Hipple, "1992: Job market in the doldrums," *Monthly Labor Review*, February, 1993, 3-14.

[2]   Kenneth Labich, "The New Unemployed," *Fortune*, March, 8, 1993, 40.

[3]   Michael Douglas, *Wall Street*, 20th Century Fox Studios, 1987.

[4]   Eugenie Allen, "Best News Ever For Working Women," *Working Woman*, February, 1993, 198.

[5]   John Balzas, "U.S. Work Force in Transition," *Los Angeles Times*, April 7, 1993, A1.

[6]   John A. Byrne, "Paradigms for Postmodern Managers," *BusinessWeek/Reinventing America*, 1992, 62.

[7]   Allen, "Best News Ever," 198.

[8]   Linda Grant, "Breaking The Mold: Companies Struggle to Reinvent Themselves," *Los Angeles Times*, May 3, 1992, D1.

[9]   Ibid.

Chapter 2

[1] Walter Kiechel III, "How We Will Work In The Year 2000," *Fortune*, May 17,1993, 38.

[2] Carol J. Loomis, "Dinosaurs?," *Fortune*, May 3, 1993, 36.

[3] Michael Hammer and James Champy, "Reengineering the Corporation: A Manifesto for Business Revolution," Fortune Book Excerpt, *Fortune*, May 3, 1993, 94.

[4] Lance Morrow, "The Temping of America," *Time*, March 29, 1993, 47.

[5] Shawn Tully, "The Modular Corporation," *Fortune*, February 8, 1993, 106.

[6] Peter Burrows, "Farming Out Work—To IBM, DEC, NCR . . .," *BusinessWeek*, May 17, 1993, 92.

[7] Charles Handy, *The Age of Unreason* (Boston: Harvard Business School Press, 1989), 90-94.

[8] Burrows, "Farming Out Work," 92.

[9] John Huey, "Corporate Culture Shock: An IBM-Apple Computer Joint Venture," *Fortune*, April 5, 1993, 38.

[10] Balzas, "U.S. Work Force in Transition," A1.

[11] Myron Magnet, "Why Job Growth Is Stalled," *Fortune*, March 8, 1993, 51.

[12] John Greenwald, "The Great American Layoffs," *Time*, July 20, 1992, 64.

[13] Magnet, "Why Job Growth Is Stalled," 51.

[14] Brian O'Reilly, "Your New Global Work Force," *Fortune*, December, 14, 1992, 52.

[15] Magnet, "Why Job Growth Is Stalled," 51.

[16] Ibid.

[17] Balzas, "U.S. Work Force in Transition," A1.

[18] Marilyn Moats Kennedy, "Job Strategies: Smart moves for bumpy times," *Glamour*, October, 1991, 113.

[19] Handy, *The Age of Unreason*, 183-185.

[20] Morrow, "The Temping of America," 47.

Chapter 3

1   Marlys Harris, "What's wrong with this picture?," *Working Woman*, December, 1990, 72.

2   Sue McKibbin, Ph.D., "Doing What You Love," *Shape*, November, 1990, 46.

3   Shena Crane, "Yesterday's job search strategy no longer works," *Orange County Business Journal*, May 4-10, 1992, 12.

4   Jonathan Peterson, "The Path to Success Isn't On a Ladder," *Los Angeles Times*, September 16, 1991, A1.

5   Ayala Pines and Elliot Aronson, *Career Burnout Causes & Cures*, (New York: The Free Press, 1989), 11.

6   Laurie Peterson, "Lower Your Expectations," *ADWEEK's Marketing Week*, November 26, 1990, 18.

Chapter 4

1   Greenwald, "The Great American Layoffs," *Time*, 64.

2   Carl T. Hall, San Francisco Chronicle, "White-collar wages falling, report says," *Orange County Register*, September 7, 1992, A1.

3   Hage, "White Collar Wasteland," 42.

4   Terms from: (1) "These Buzz Words Imply a Buzz Saw," *Orange County Register*, August 24, 1991; (2) Alan Gathright, Knight-Ridder Newspapers, "The language of layoffs: Companies search for soft words for hard times," *Orange County Register*, February 16, 1992, K5.

5   Dana Parsons, "The Jobless White-Collar Worker—a Fish Out of Water," *Los Angeles Times*, April 17, 1991, B1.

6   Tom Post, "The civilized way to fire an employee," *Self*, April, 1992, 105.

7   Karen Astrid Larson, "Job Jitters," *Working Mother*, February, 1993, 28.

8   Perri Capell, "Endangered Middle Man," *American Demographics*, January, 1992, 44.

9   David J. Lynch, "Hughes' severance criticized," *Orange County Register*, August, 1992, D1.

[10]   James W. Hunt, *The Law of the Workplace, Rights of Employer and Employees,* Second Edition, (Washington, D.C.: The Bureau of National Affairs, Inc., n.d.) 48.

[11]   Ellen Forman, Fort Lauderdale Sun-Sentinel, "Neuroses developed in past can haunt job," *Orange County Register,* F2.

[12]   Kathleen Murray, "Life after a layoff," *Orange County Register,* August 1, 1990, K1.

[13]   Study results from: (1) "Writing Helps," *Wall Street Journal,* December, 1, 1992, A1; (2) Kelly Good McGee, "Writing Off the Pain of Job Loss," *New Woman,* June, 1992, n.p.

[14]   Parsons, "The Jobless White-Collar Worker," B1.

[15]   Labich, "The New Unemployed," 40.

[16]   Parsons, "The Jobless White-Collar Worker," B1.

[17]   Sharon E. Barnes and D.M. Pusateri, "Lean On Me," *Executive Female,* May/June, 1991, 53.

[18]   Dr. Lee Salk, "Tough Times," *McCall's,* June, 1991, 81.

[19]   Howard Goldberg, The Associated Press, "Anxiety: Workers wary of layoffs," *Orange County Register,* February 6, 1993, C3.

[20]   Patrick Houston, "Surviving the Survivor Syndrome," *Working Woman,* August, 1992, 57.

[21]   "Workplace stress is rampant, especially with recession," *Wall Street Journal,* June 5, 1992, 1.

[22]   Houston, "Surviving the Survivor Syndrome," 57.

[23]   Christopher Conte, "Downsizing Hurts," *Wall Street Journal,* September 15, 1992, A1.

[24]   Houston, "Surviving the Survivor Syndrome," 57.

[25]   Ibid.

[26]   Mark Stevens, "Recession Anxiety?," *Executive Female,* March/April, 1992, 25.

Chapter 5

[1]   Karen Tumulty, "The Dead-End Kids," *Los Angeles Times,* October 28, 1990, 10.

2   Joseph H. Boyett and Henry P. Conn, *Workplace 2000: The Revolution Reshaping American Business*, (New York: Penguin Group, 1991), 29.

3   Joseph Weber, Lisa Driscoll, Richard Brandt, bureau reports, "Farewell, Fast Track," *BusinessWeek*, December 10, 1990, 192.

4   Peter Drucker, "The New Society of Organizations," *Harvard Business Review*, September/October, 1992, 95.

5   Linda Grant, "Recipe for Survival," *Los Angeles Times*, May 31, 1992, D1.

6   Jim Jubak, "The New Work Rules for the '90s," *REDBOOK*, December, 1992, 46.

7   Mark Alpert, "The Care and Feeding of Engineers," *Fortune*, September 21, 1992, 87.

8   Grant, "Breaking the Mold," D1.

9   Handy, *The Age of Unreason*, 279.

10 Drucker, "The New Society of Organizations," 95.

11 John Labate, "What's Wrong With Workers?," *Fortune*, August 10, 1992, 18.

12 Grant, "Breaking the Mold," D1.

13 Kelly Good McGee, "Careerwise," *New Woman*, August, 1992, 36.

14 Alpert, "The Care and Feeding of Engineers," 86.

15 Kenneth Labich, "The New Pay Game . . . And How You Measure Up," *Fortune*, October 19, 1992, 114.

16 Donald Woutat, "Detroit's Struggle to Shift Gears," *Los Angeles Times*, May 30, 1992, A1.

17 Christopher Conte, "Self-Directed Work Gains Popularity," *Wall Street Journal*, February 12, 1993, A1.

18 Grant, "Breaking the Mold," D1.

19 Handy, *The Age of Unreason*, 153-155.

20 David Kirkpatrick, "Could AT&T Rule The World?," *Fortune*, May 17, 1993, 55.

21   Handy, *The Age of Unreason,* 134.

22   Noel M. Tichy, Stratford Sherman, "Jack Welch's Lessons For Success," Fortune Book Excerpt, *Fortune,* January 25, 1993, 86.

23   Marina N. Ruderman, "Who Gets Promoted?," *Executive Female,* May/June 1992, 33.

24   R. Craig MacLaren, "Compensation Practices Mirror Changes in Business Realities," *Promo: The International Magazine for Promotional Marketing,* April, 1992, 43.

25   Joan E. Rigdon, "Using Lateral Moves to Spur Employees," *Wall Street Journal,* May 26, 1992, B1.

26   MacLaren, "Compensation Practices Mirror Changes in Business Realities," 43.

27   Kenny Rogers, *The Gambler,* Hal Leonard, 1977.

28   Frank Herbert, *Dune,* (New York: Ace Books, 1965), 8.

Chapter 6

1   Stephen Franklin, Chicago Tribune, " '92 Pay Raises Were a Record Low 3.7%," *Orange County Register,* January 2, 1992, C1.

2   "Many Firms Give Up on 5% Pay Raises," *Wall Street Journal,* November 7, 1992, A1.

3   Boyett, *Workplace 2000,* 118.

4   Hall, "White-collar wages falling, report says," 16.

5   Rosabeth Moss Kanter, *When Giants Learn to Dance,* (New York: Simon and Schuster, 1989), 229.

6   Labich, "The New Pay Game," 115.

7   Brian O'Reily, "How To Murder The Competition," *Fortune,* February 22, 1993, 87.

8   Labich, "The New Pay Game," 115.

9   MacClaren, "Compensation Practices Mirror Changes in Business Realities," 43.

10   Hank Ezell, Cox News Service, "Plans putting performance into paychecks," *Orange County Register,* C2.

11 "Linking Directors' Pay To Companies' Fortunes," *Wall Street Journal*, October 13, 1992, A1.

12 Kanter, *When Giants Learn to Dance*, 259.

13 Ezell, "Plans putting performance into paychecks," C2.

14 MacClaren, "Compensation Practices Mirror Changes in Business Realities," 43.

15 Ezell, "Plans putting performance into paychecks," C2.

16 Albert R. Karr, "Labor Letter: A Special News Report on People and Their Jobs in Office, Fields, and Factories," *Wall Street Journal*, June 13, 1992, 10.

17 Ibid.

18 MacClaren, "Compensation Practices Mirror Changes in Business Realities," 43.

19 Melissa Wahl, "Where To Dig Dirt on Salaries," *Executive Female*, May/June, 1992, 69.

20 Christopher Caggiano, "What Do Workers Want?," *Inc.*, November, 1992, 101.

21 MacClaren, "Compensation Practices Mirror Changes in Business Realities," 43.

22 Susan Moffat, "Fewer workers have health insurance," *Los Angeles Times*, January 23,1992, D1.

23 "Vacations for sale, or to buy: Many workers like the idea," *Wall Street Journal*, August 2, 1992, A1.

24 Orlando Sentinel, "Some companies offer employees legal-advice plans as benefit," *Orange County Register*, November 9, 1992.

25 Ann Hornday, "Work perks . . . the next best thing to making more money," *American Woman*, n.d., 9.

26 Ibid.

27 Labich, "The New Pay Game," 115.

Chapter 7

1   Christopher Farrell, Michael Mandel, Michael Schroeder, Joseph Weber, Michael Galen, Gary McWilliams, "The Economic Crisis of Urban America," *BusinessWeek*, May 18, 1992, 38.

2   Jean Merl, "High-Tech Aim to Prepare Workers of Future," *Los Angeles Times*, May 13, 1991, 13.

3   Boyett, *Workplace 2000*, 276.

4   Handy, *The Age of Unreason*, 34-35.

5   Rosanne Keynan, "Happiness At Work, Like a Good Marriage, It Requires Real Effort," *Los Angeles Times*, September 16, 1991, 7.

6   Boyett, *Workplace 2000*, 271.

7   Steven Greenhouse, "The Coming Crisis of the American Work Force," *New York Times*, June 7, 1992, 1-4.

8   Ray Marshall and Marc Tucker, *Thinking For A Living*, (New York: BasicBooks, A Division of HarperCollins Publishers, 1992), xviii.

9   Howard Muson, "Schooled for Success," *Working Woman*, January, 1993, 33.

10   Tamara Henry, Associated Press, "Group calls for program to boost worker literacy," *Orange County Register*, B1.

11   Alan Deutshman, "Why Kids Should Learn About Work," *Fortune*, August 10, 1992, 86.

12   Boyett, *Workplace 2000*, 268.

13   Farrell, "The Economic Crisis of Urban America," 38.

14   Louis S. Richman, "Struggling to Save Our Kids," *Fortune*, August 10, 1992, 34.

15   Carol Kleinman, *The 100 Best Job$ for the 1990s & Beyond*, (Chicago: Dearborn Financial Publishing, Inc., 1992), 4.

16   Brian O'Reily, "The Job Drought," *Fortune*, August 24, 1992, 62.

17   Paula Mergenbagen, "Doing the Career Shuffle," *American Demographics*, November, 1991, 42.

18   Ken Dychtwald, Ph.D. and Joe Flower, *Age Wave: How the Most Important Trend of Our Time Will Change Your Future*, (New York: Bantam Books, 1990), 98.

19   Kleinman, *The 100 Best Job$ for the 1990s & Beyond*, 32-33.

20   Ibid, 36.

21   Ibid, 38-39.

22   Mark Alpert, "The Care and Feeding of Engineers," *Fortune*, September 21, 1992, 86.

23   Gene Koretz, "College Grads Find Fewer Jobs—And Now, For Less Pay," *BusinessWeek*, March 22, 1993, 22.

24   B.J. Roche, "It's Never Too Late To Go Back To School," *New Woman*, September, 1992, 126.

25   Ibid.

26   Kleinman, *The 100 Best Job$ for the 1990s & Beyond*, 34.

27   Ibid, 34-35.

28   O'Reilly, "The Job Drought," 62.

29   Graduate School of Management Program, University of California at Irvine.

30   John Elson, "Campus of the Future," *Time*, April 13, 1992, 54.

31   Ibid.

32   John A. Byrne, "Weekend Warriors: A Guide to MBA's for Working Executives," *BusinessWeek*, October 28, 1991, 109.

33   Michael Flagg, "MBA Locomotive Losing Some Steam," *Los Angeles Times*, September 30, 1991, D10.

34   Mary Lord, "The M.B.A. Gets Real," *U.S. News & World Report*, March 22, 1993, 54.

35   Cyndee Miller, "MBA Boom Goes Bust," *Marketing News*, March 2, 1992.

36   Roche, "It's Never Too Late to go Back to School," 126.

37   Jennifer Reese, "Michigan's Real-World MBAs," *Fortune*, June 3-14, 1993, 11.

38   Lord, "The M.B.A. Gets Real," 54.

39   Miller, "MBA Boom Goes Bust," 1.

40   Susan Dentzer, "How to Train Workers for the 21st Century," *U.S. News & World Report*, September 21, 1992, 72.

41   Ronald Henkoff, "Companies That Train Best," *Fortune*, March 22, 1993, 62.

42   Marshall, *Thinking For A Living*, 51.

43   Noel M. Tichy, Stratford Sherman, "Control Your Destiny," Fortune Book Excerpt, *Fortune*, January 25, 1993, 86.

44   Ronald Henkoff, "Where Will The Jobs Come From?," *Fortune*, October 19, 1992, 58.

45   Dentzer, "How to Train Workers for the 21st Century," 72.

46   Matt Rothman, "Into the Black," *Inc.*, January, 1993, 59.

47   Thomas A. Stewart, "U.S. Productivity: First But Fading," *Fortune*, October 19, 1992, 54.

48   Henkoff, "Companies That Train Best," 62.

49   Brian O'Reily, "How Execs Learn Now," *Fortune*, April 5, 1993, 52.

Chapter 8

1   Bob Cooper, "There's No Place Like Home," *VisaVis—The World Brought to You by United Airlines*, September, 1992, 44.

2   James E. Ellis, Christina Del Valley, "Tall Order for Small Businesses," *BusinessWeek*, April 19, 1993, 114.

3   Ronni Sandroff, "Are Small Companies Better?," *Working Mother*, November, 1992, 34.

4   Boyett, *Workplace 2000*, 41.

5   Marilyn Moats Kennedy, "The Pros and Cons of Working for A Small Company," *Glamour*, July, 1992, 79.

6   Ellis, "Tall Order for Small Businesses," 114.

7   Sandroff, "Are Small Companies Better?," 34.

8   Cooper, "There's No Place Like Home," 44.

9   Ibid.

10   Ibid.

[11] Ibid.

[12] Marc Myers, "The Truth About Telecommuting," *Working Woman*, March, 1992, 17.

[13] Diane Cole, "New Corporate Pioneers?," *New Woman*, November, 1991, 90.

[14] Cooper, "There's No Place Like Home," 44.

[15] Deborah Baroset Diamond, "A Great Place to Work," *Ladies Home Journal*, May, 1992, 100.

[16] Cole, "New Corporate Pioneers?," 90.

[17] Leslie Berkman, "There's No Workplace Like Home," *Los Angeles Times*, April 16, 1991, D9.

[18] Jane Ciabattari, "Job Market Fall Out," *Working Woman*, December, 1991, 65.

[19] Julie Rose, "More Part-Time, But Not By Choice," *Los Angeles Times*, September 6, 1991, 25.

[20] Eugenie Allen, "Best News Ever for Working Women," *Time*, May, 1991, 198.

[21] Ibid.

[22] Rose, "More Part-Time, But Not By Choice," 25.

[23] Martha Groves, Michael Granberry, "B of A Tellers Get Squeezed," *Los Angeles Times*, February 6, 1991, D1.

[24] Marlys Harris, "Labor Pains," *Lear's*, May, 1993, 18.

[25] Laura Fisher, "Executive Temping: Too Good to be True," *Working Woman*, April, 1992, 21.

[26] Harris, "Labor Pains," 18.

[27] Janice Castro, "Disposable Workers," *Time*, March 29, 1993, 43.

[28] Kathleen Murray, "Hiring By Contract: Trend of the '90s," *Orange County Register*, March 8, 1992, 4.

[29] Martin Booe, "Working Free Can Still Pay Off," *Los Angeles Times*, March 1, 1992, 19.

[30] Labich, "The New Unemployed," 40.

[31] Agencies cited from: (1) Janice Castro, "Disposable Workers," *Time*, March, 29, 1993, 43; (2), Jill Bettner,

"Test-Tube Temps Fill Lab Needs," *Los Angeles Times*, May 31, 1993, D2.

Chapter 9

1   Jane Applegate, "From Executive to Entrepreneur," *Working Woman*, July, 1992, 33.

2   Ibid.

3   Tom Post, "Shifting Out of Career Limbo," *Self*, May, 1992, 86.

4   Ibid.

5   Tumulty, "The Dead-End Kids," 10.

6   Patrick Houston, "Sell what you know," *Self*, March, 1992, 129.

7   Bruce Nussbaum, Alice Cuneo, Barbara Carlson, Gary Williams, "Corporate Refugees, After the Pain, Some Find Smooth Sailing," *BusinessWeek*, April 12, 1993, 58.

8   Houston, "Sell what you know," 129.

9   Nussbaum, "Corporate Refugees," 58.

10 Michelle Galen, Laurel Trouby, Lori Bongiorno, Wendy Zellner, "Franchise Fracas," *BusinessWeek*, March 22, 1993, 68.

11 Kathy M. Kristof, "What to Look for When You Check Out Franchises," *Los Angeles Times*, September, 1992, D10.

12 Ibid.

13 Galen, "Franchise Fracas," 68.

14 Kanter, *When Giants Learn To Dance*, 314-315.

15 Ibid.

16 Diamond, "A Great Place to Work," 10.

17 J. Robert Connor, *Cracking the Over-50 Job Market*, (New York: Penguin Group, 1992), 203.

18 Applegate, "From Executive to Entrepreneur," 33.

19 Kristof, "What to Look for When You Check out Franchises," D10.

20 Kleinman, *The 100 Best Job$ for the 1990s & Beyond*, 112.

21 Leslie Brokaw, "The Truth About Start-Ups," *Inc.*, March, 1993, 56.

22 Applegate, "From Executive to Entrepreneur," 33.

23 Connor, *Cracking the Over-50 Job Market*, 212.

24 Kleinman, *The 100 Best Job$ for the 1990s & Beyond*, 114.

25 Ibid.

26 Kate Betrand, "Home Is Where the Office Is," *Business Marketing*, February, 1991, 9.

27 Cooper, "There's No Place Like Home," 44.

28 Ibid.

29 Kleinman, *The 100 Best Job$ for the 1990s & Beyond*, 114-115.

30 Cooper, "There's No Place Like Home," 44.

31 Ibid.

32 Laurel Touby, "Starting a Business on the Side," *Working Woman*, September, 1992, 44.

33 Applegate, "From Executive to Entrepreneur," 33.

Chapter 10

1 Lisa J. Moore, "An Argument For Starting Small," *U.S. News & World Report*, October 26, 1992, 85.

2 On-campus recruiting data from: (1) Kristina A. Lindgren, "Job Search is Hard Work for O.C. Graduates," *Los Angeles Times*, May 31, 1992, A1; (2) Bobbie Browning, Q & A, *Los Angeles Times*, May 11, 1992, D4.

3 Moore, "An Argument For Starting Small," 85.

4 Lindgren, "Job Search Is Hard Work for O.C. Graduates," A1.

5 *Newsweek* Interview with Jack Welch, "He Brought GE to Life," *Newsweek*, November 30, 1992, 62.

6 Myron Brenton, "Why Should They Hire You—A Dime-a-Dozen New Grad?," *Cosmopolitan Life After College*, Spring, 1992, 78.

7   Nina J. Easton, "McFuture Shock," *Los Angeles Time*, June 7, 1992, 22.

8   Judith Newman, "Growing up is hard to do . . . But here's how to fake it," *Cosmopolitan Life After College*, Spring, 1992, 66.

9   "How I Landed My Great Job: 19 Success Stories," *Cosmopolitan Life After College*, Spring, 1993, 14.

10   Julie Amparano Lopez, "College Class of '93 Learns Hard Lesson: Career Prospects Are Worst in Decades," *Wall Street Journal*, May 20, 1993, B1.

11   Associated Press, "New Graduates Face a Hard Time This Year," The Southern California Job Market, *Los Angeles Times*, March 1, 1993, 7.

12   Dan Froomkin, "Job-hunting grads find it rough out there," *Orange County Register*, May 10,1992, C1.

13   Bobbie Browning, Q & A, D4.

14   Sherri Hershkowitz, "What I Wish I'd Known," *Cosmopolitan Life After College*, Spring, 1992, 115.

15   Newman, "Growing up is hard to do . . . But here's how to fake it," 66.

16   Byron De Arakal, "Where to Now?," *Orange County Metropolitan*, June 1, 1992, 13.

17   Easton, "McFuture Shock," 22.

18   Moore, "An Argument For Starting Small," 85.

19   "How I Landed My Great Job: 19 Success Stories," 14.

20   Ibid.

21   Bobbie Browning, Q & A, D4.

22   Hershkowitz, "What I Wish I'd Known," 115.

23   Easton, "McFuture Shock," 22.

24   Moore, "An Argument For Starting Small," 85.

25   Ibid.

26   Ibid.

27   Labor Letter, *Wall Street Journal*, n.d., A1.

28 Hershkowitz, "What I Wish I'd Known," 115.

29 Brenton, "Why Should They Hire You—A Dime-a-Dozen New Grad?," 78.

30 Ibid.

31 Hershkowitz, "What I Wish I'd Known," 115.

32 Brenton,"Why Should They Hire You—A Dime-a-Dozen New Grad?," 78.

33 Ibid.

34 De Arakal, "Where to Now?," 13.

35 Barry M. Horstman, Jennifer Toth, "Answer to Idealism or Joblessness," *Los Angeles Times*, August, 1992, A1.

36 Ibid.

37 Ibid.

38 Ibid.

39 Ibid.

40 Ibid.

41 Ibid.

42 Michael Winkelman, "The Grad-School Question," *Cosmopolitan Life After College*, Spring, 1993, 50.

43 Paul Lim, "Some New Grads Turn Entrepreneur, Not Employee," *Wall Street Journal*, June 25, 1992, A2.

44 Ibid.

45 Lindgren, "Job Search Is Hard Work For O.C. Graduates," A1.

46 Judith Waldrop, "The First Job," *American Demographics*, June, 1992, 4.

47 Winkelman, "The Grad-School Question," 50.

48 "Oh, the Places We'll Go!," *Cosmopolitan Life After College*, Spring, 1993, 138.

Chapter 11

1 Data from: (1) Gene Koretz, "Grimmer Job-Loss Numbers for America's Defense Industry, Economic Trends,"

BusinessWeek, June 7, 1993; (2) Melissa Healy, Glenn F. Bunting and Dwight Morris, "Big Guns Aren't Sole Casualties," *Los Angeles Times*, May 23, 1993, A1.

2   Stephen Budiansky, "Flying blind into a turbulent future," *U.S. News & World Report*, December 7, 1992, 58.

3   Irene Sage, Boston Globe, "Baby Boom Generation Hits Snag," *Orange County Register*, January 7, 1992, E1.

4   Ralph Vartabedian, "Fair Chance at Jobs," *Los Angeles Times*, May 16, 1992, D1.

5   Eric Schine, Amy Borrus, John Carey, Geoffrey Smith and bureau reports, "The Defense Whizzes Making It In Civvies," *BusinessWeek*, September 7, 1992, 88.

6   Ibid.

7   Amy Borrus, Eric Schine, Zachary Schiller, Lisa Driscoll, Joseph Weber, "From Bullets to Bullet Trains: It Won't Be Easy," *BusinessWeek*, April 20, 1992, 110.

8   Ibid.

9   Ronald Shrinkman, "Rockwell Joins 'Smart Highway' Technology Race," *Orange County Business Journal*, January 25, 1993, 3.

10   Amy Borrus, "From Bullets to Bullet Trains: It Won't Be Easy," 110.

11   Ibid.

12   Susan Moffat, "Healing the State's Ailing Job Market," *Los Angeles Times*, January 24, 1993, D1.

13   David J. Lynch, "Rockwell Shifts Gears," *Orange County Register*, January 12, 1993, C1.

14   Eric Schine, Kathleen Kerwin, "Hughes Bets On Another Kind of Bird," *BusinessWeek*, November 9, 1992, 65.

15   Schine, "The Defense Whizzes Making It In Civvies," 88.

16   Ralph Vartabedian, "Flying in the Face of Turbulence," *Los Angeles Times*, December 4, 1992, A1.

17   Borrus, "From Bullets to Bullet Trains: It Won't Be Easy," 110.

18   Schine, "The Defense Whizzes Making It In Civvies," 88.

19   Budiansky, "Flying blind into a turbulent future," 58.

20   Schine, "The Defense Whizzes Making It In Civvies," 88.

21   Budiansky, "Flying blind into a turbulent future," 58.

22   Ibid.

23   Lynch, "Rockwell Shifts Gears," C1.

24   Budiansky, "Flying blind into a turbulent future," 58.

25   Tom Gorman, "Getting a Life After Aerospace," *Los Angeles Times*, March 5, 1993, A1.

26   Ibid.

27   Ibid.

Chapter 12

1   "Hot Gadgets For Disabled Workers," *American Demographics*, January, 1993, 23.

2   Charles Green, Knight-Ridder Newspapers, "Laws to protect disabled slow to crack barriers," *Orange County Register*, June 26,1993, 2.

3   Jan Jaben, "Enabling the Disabled," *Business Marketing*, July, 1992, 24.

4   Americans With Disabilities Act of 1990.

5   Interview with Miriam Whitfield, Program Director with Social Vocational Services in Los Angeles, California; conducted by Judy Cooper, April, 1992.

6   Interviews with Barbara Haney, Director of Community Resources with Employ America in Los Angeles, California; conducted by Judy Cooper, April, 1992.

7   "Willing and Able: Americans With Disabilities in the New Work Force," *BusinessWeek*, October 28, 1991, 37.

8   Ibid

9   Ibid.

10   Ibid.

11   Ibid.

[12]   Haney interview, April, 1992.

[13]   Andrea Maier, "Enabling Disabled," *Los Angeles Times*, July 24, 1992, D1.

[14]   Ibid.

[15]   Mary Lord, "Away with barriers," *U.S. News & World Report*, July 20, 1992, 60.

[16]   "Willing and Able: Americans With Disabilities in the New Work Force," 37.

[17]   Resources from materials for disabled workers provided by Employ America.

[18]   "Willing and Able: Americans With Disabilities in the New Work Force," 37.

[19]   Materials from Just One Break, Inc. (J.O.B.), New York, New York.

[20]   Ibid

[21]   Ibid.

[22]   Ibid.

[23]   Ibid.

[24]   Joann S. Lublin, "Disabilities Act Will Compel Businesses To Change Many Employment Practices," *Wall Street Journal*, August, 1992, A1.

[25]   "Willing and Able: Americans With Disabilities in the New Work Force," 37.

[26]   Ibid.

[27]   Ibid.

[28]   Ibid.

[29]   Whitfield interview, April, 1992.

[30]   Christopher Conte, "Compliance costs are often modest under the new disability law," *Wall Street Journal*, August 24, 1992, A1.

[31]   Maier, "Enabling Disabled," D1.

[32]   Jack Anderson, Parade, "Language of Hope," *Reader's Digest*, February, 1993, 24.

Chapter 13

1   Robert A. Rosenblatt, "2.5 Million Arms Jobs Are at Risk," *Los Angeles Times*, February 22, 1992, D1.

2   Melissa Healy, "A New Set of Marching Orders," *Los Angeles Times*, November 2, 1992, A1.

3   Melissa Healy, "Battling Life After The Service," *Los Angeles Times*, June 1, 1992, A1.

4   Melissa Healy, "Military Combat Retreats Into Job Market," *Los Angeles Times*, February 23, 1992, A1.

5   Ibid.

6   Ibid.

7   Ibid.

8   Ibid.

9   Ibid.

10   Ibid.

11   Ibid.

12   Ibid.

13   Ibid.

Chapter 14

1   Thomas G. Exter, "The Declining Majority," *American Demographics*, January, 1993, 59.

2   Robert A. Rosenblatt, "A Shortage of Skills? Analysts Fear Minorities' Education Won't Keep Pace," *Los Angeles Times*, June 1, 1993, D1.

3   Steven D. Kaye, "A New Interest in Cracking the Glass Ceiling," *U.S. News & World Report*, October 26, 1992, 80.

4   Renu Sehgal, Boston Globe, "Study says top of corporate ladder still a far reach for women, minorities," *Orange County Register*, August 9, 1991, D1.

5   Ibid.

6   E. Wynter, "Minority Directors Remain a Rare Breed," *Wall Street Journal*, n.d., A1.

7   Information forum: Diversity Task, Pacific Bell's Consumer Advisory Council XII, 1990-1992.

8   Kaye, "A New Interest in Cracking the Glass Ceiling," 80.

9   Ibid.

10   Ibid.

11   Alice Cuneo, "Diverse by Design," *BusinessWeek/ Reinventing America*, 1992, 72.

12   Kaye, "A New Interest in Cracking the Glass Ceiling," 80.

13   Ellyn E. Spragins, "Managing Diversity," *Inc.*, January, 1993, 33.

14   Kristina Lindgren, "UCI Extension Puts Accent on Ethnic Training," *Los Angeles Times*, April 12, 1992, B1.

15   Jeaannye Thorton, David Whitman, Dorian Friedman, "White myths about blacks," *U.S. News & World Report*, November 9, 1993, 41.

16   Michael Meyer, "Los Angeles 2010: A Latino Subcontinent," *Newsweek*, November 9, 1992, 32.

17   "More blacks moving into white-collar jobs," *Orange County Register*, December 9, 1992, C1.

18   Simson L. Garfinkel, "Shortage of Scientists Sends Signals," *The Christian Science Monitor*, March 6, 1990, 12.

19   Sandra Sugwara, "Breaking Technology's Other Barriers," *The Washington Post*, August 19, 1991, 1.

20   Ralph Vartabedian, "Aerospace Careers in Low Orbit," *Los Angeles Times*, November 16, 1992, A1.

21   Ibid.

22   Bob Cox, Knight Ridder Newspapers, "A Bright Idea, Taking Advantage of Workers' Differences," *Orange County Register*, December 14, 1992, D1.

23   "Women, Minorities Own More Small Businesses," *Wall Street Journal*, August 12, 1992, B1.

24   J. Bruce Llewelyn, ". . . It Won't Be Easy, But Go Out and Do It," Ideas for the '90s, *Fortune*, March 26, 1990, 52.

Chapter 15

1   MacClaren, "Compensation Practices Mirror Changes in Business Realities," 43.

2   Christopher Conte, "Early retirement offers remains popular cost-cutting method," *Wall Street Journal*, August 25, 1992, A1.

3   David Kirkpatrick, "Breaking Up IBM," *Fortune*, July 27, 1992, 44.

4   Copley News Service, "Age when baby boomers say they would like to retire," *Orange County Register*, June 7, 1992, R7.

5   Irene Sege, The Boston Globe, "Baby boom generation hits snags," *Orange County Register*, January 7, 1992, E1.

6   Dychtwald, *Age Wave*, 175.

7   Linda Grant, "Fired at Fifty," *Los Angeles Times*, September 22, 1992, D1.

8   Sherry Angel, "Older Job Seekers Have Their Work Cut Out," *Los Angeles Times*, April 26, 1991, A1.

9   Grant, "Fired at Fifty," D1.

10   Ibid.

11   Conte, "Early retirement offers remains popular cost-cutting method," A1.

12   Patricia O'Toole, "Age Bias in the Workplace: Flight Begins at 40," *Lear's*, May, 1992, 22.

13   Dychtwald, *Age Wave*, 175.

14   Ibid, 30.

15   "Economic Trends," *BusinessWeek*, November 11, 1992, 53.

16   Dychtwald, *Age Wave*, 42.

17   O'Toole, "Age Bias in the Workplace: Flight Begins at 40," 22.

18   Dychtwald, *Age Wave*, 42.

19   Ibid.

20   Sherry Angel, "Older Job Seekers Have Their Work Cut Out," *Los Angeles Times*, April 4, 1991, E1.

21   Ibid.

22   Lisa J. Moore and Michael J. Newman, "Still Working," *U.S. News & World Report*, May 25, 1992, 80.

23   Register News Service, "Life after a career," *Orange County Register*, February 22, 1993, D4.

24   O'Toole, "Age Bias in the Workplace: Flight Begins at 40," 22.

25   Kleinman, *The 100 Best Job$ for the '90s & Beyond*, 11.

26   Caroline Bird, *Second Careers: New Ways to Work After 50*, (Boston: Little, Brown and Company), 1992.

27   Angel, "Older Job Seekers Have Their Work Cut Out," E1.

Chapter 16

1   Maggie Mahar, "The Truth About Women's Pay," *Working Woman*, April, 1993, 52.

2   Donna K.H. Walters, "Gender Gap Narrowing as Men's Pay Drops at Faster Rate Than Women's Pay," *Los Angeles Times*, September 13, 1992, D3.

3   Amanda Troy Segal, Wendy Zelner, and bureau reports, "Corporate Women," *BusinessWeek*, May 8, 1992, 74.

4   Andrea Shalai-Esa, Reuters, "Study: 'Glass Ceiling' still intact," *Orange County Register*, August 12, 1992, C3.

5   Ibid.

6   Walters, "Gender Gap Narrowing as Men's Pay Drops at Faster Rate Than Women's Pay," D3.

7   Joan E. Rigdon, "Three Decades After the Equal Pay Act, Women's Wages Remain Far From Parity," *Wall Street Journal*, June 9, 1993, B1.

[8]   Segal, "Corporate Women," 74.

[9]   Catherine Romano, "Six Million Women: Two at the Top," *Working Woman*, June, 1993, 15.

[10]   Ann M. Morrison, Randall P. White, Ellen Van Veslor and the Center for Creative Leadership, *Breaking The Glass Ceiling*, (Massachusetts: Addison-Wesley, 1987).

[11]   Renu Sehgal, Boston Globe, "Study says top of corporate ladder still a far reach for women, minorities," *Orange County Register*, August 9, 1991, C1.

[12]   Segal, "Corporate Women," 74.

[13]   Patricia Aburdene and John Naisbitt, *Megatrends for Women*, (New York: Villard Books, 1992), xvi.

[14]   Segal, "Corporate Women," 74.

[15]   Susan Merrell, "When a Woman Manages the Company," Career, *New Woman*, January, 1993, 112.

[16]   Jill Andresky Fraser, "Women Power in the New Age," *Working Woman*, December, 1992, 59.

[17]   Donna Jackson, "Shattering The Glass Ceiling," *New Woman*, September, 1992, 146.

[18]   Michele Morris, "Why It Doesn't Pay To Be A Good Girl," *Executive Female*, May/June, 1993, 48.

[19]   Lynne S. Dumas, "Catapult Your Career!" *New Woman*, June, 1993, 124.

[20]   Priscilla Painton, "The Maternal Wall," *Time*, May 10, 1993, 42.

[21]   Kelly Good McGee, "Money and the Mommy Track," *New Woman*, September, 1992, 40.

[22]   Painton, "The Maternal Wall," 42.

[23]   Ibid.

[24]   Julie Amparano Lopez, "Career women are being helped more, and in new ways, when jobs turn sour," *Wall Street Journal*, July 3, 1992, A1.

[25]   Ibid.

[26]   Ibid.

27   Joann S. Lublin, "Husbands in Limbo," *Wall Street Journal*, April 13, 1993, 1.

28   Fraser, "Women Power in the New Age," 59.

29   Aburdene, *Megatrends for Women*, 62.

30   Statistics from: (1) Lynn Povich, "Letter From The Editor," *Working Woman*, May, 1992, 14; (2) Nam Nguyen, "How Women-Owned Businesses Fare," *Orange County Register*, April 14, 1992, C1.

31   Segal, "Corporate Women," 74.

32   Houston, "Sell what you know," 129.

33   Faye Fiore, "Women's Career-Family Juggling Act: Corporations Are Taking Notice," *Los Angeles Times*, December 13, 1992, D3.

Chapter 17

1   Hage, "White Collar Wasteland," 42.

2   Labor Letter, A1.

3   Ibid.

4   Catherine Romano, "Write the Perfect Résumé!," *Cosmopolitan Life After College*, Spring, 1992, 38.

5   Marilyn Moats Kennedy, "Should you lie to get a job?," *Glamour*, November, 1992, 135.

6   Greenwald, "The Great American Layoffs," 64.

7   Stuart Silverstein, "Exasperating Search for Work Takes Toll of Long-Term Jobless," *Los Angeles Times*, September 26, 1992, D3.

8   Kelly Good McGee, "Job-Hunting Strategies for the 1990s," *New Woman*, December, 1992, 44.

9   Silverstein, "Exasperating Search for Work Takes Toll of Long-Term Jobless," D3.

10   Kathleen Murray, "Out of Work, But Not Out of Options, OC's Forty Plus," *Orange County Register*, January 18, 1991, C1.

11   From materials supplied by The Five O'Clock Club, and interview with Kate Wendleton, founder; conducted by

Judy Cooper, May, 1992.

[12]   Ibid.

[13]   "Job scams are on the rise," *Glamour*, March, 1992, 102.

[14]   Diane Lewis, Boston Globe, "Conning The Jobless," *Orange County Register*, June 7, 1993, B6.

[15]   Alexandra Siegel, "Beware: Job Hunting Rip-Offs," *Working Woman*, January, 1992, 14.

[16]   Ibid.

[17]   "Job scams are on the rise," 102.

[18]   Kathy M. Kristof, "Paying for No Paycheck," *Los Angeles Times*, December 2, 1992, D1.

[19]   Rosch, "The ten biggest blunders of anxious job hunters," 52.

[20]   Max Edelson, "The Hottest Jobs of the 1990s," *American Demographics*, November, 1992, 14.

[21]   Ibid.

[22]   Lynne S. Dumas, "Hot Careers for the 1990s," *Working Mother*, August, 1992, 25.

[23]   Ronald Henkoff, "Winning the New Career Game," *Fortune*, July 12, 1993, 46.

PART NINE:

INDEX

INDEX

Order Form:
WHAT DO I DO NOW?
TOOL KIT

Take the next step toward career success. Order the *What Do I Do Now?* Tool Kit containing Shena Crane's best advice, methods, forms and more.

You'll receive an easy-to-use workbook filled with:

- Sample Résumés
- Résumé Worksheets
- Sample letters for:
  - answering ads
  - networking
  - setting up interviews
  - following up
- Sample reference list and reference worksheet
- Interviewing tips with questions commonly asked and a variety of answers, as well as questions to ask
- Tips for salary and benefits negotiations

☐ Please send me the *What Do I Do Now?* Tool Kit for only $7.95 including shipping, handling and tax.

Name _____

Address _____

City _____ State _____ Zip _____

Telephone Number: (_____) _____

Quantity: _____ @ $7.95 each = Total $ _____

Method of Payment:
☐ Check Enclosed *(Payable to Vista Press)*
☐ Charge my ☐ VISA ☐ Master Card
Account # _____Exp. Date _____
Signature _____

Mail to:
Vista Press, 2102 Business Center Drive, Irvine, CA 92715
For faster delivery: FAX or CALL (714) 497-9811

(Please allow four weeks for delivery.)